Lessons in Exile

Value Inquiry Book Series

VOLUME 323

Philosophy in Spain

Edited by

Stella Villarmea (*University of Alcala de Henares*)

The titles published in this series are listed at *brill.com/vibs* and *brill.com/psp*

Lessons in Exile

By

Carlos Pereda

Translated from the Spanish by

Sean Manning

BRILL
RODOPI

LEIDEN | BOSTON

Cover illustration: *Migrants* by Helen Escobedo. Used with kind permission.

The Library of Congress Cataloging-in-Publication Data is available online at http://catalog.loc.gov

Typeface for the Latin, Greek, and Cyrillic scripts: "Brill." See and download: brill.com/brill-typeface.

ISSN 0929-8436
ISBN 978-90-04-38514-6 (paperback)
ISBN 978-90-04-38515-3 (e-book)

This book is printed on acid-free paper and produced in a sustainable manner.

For Catalina Pereda,
who also knows about these things

Contents

A Map for the Road

Is it possible that within the countless exiles that have occurred throughout history there are greater lessons waiting to be learned—lessons in exile—and not just those particular experiences of particular exiles that are so frequently studied by researchers in fields like history, sociology, political science, anthropology and law? What might these lessons hope to teach us? And, if they exist, why should they concern us?

Of course, as when dealing with the vicissitudes of any social construction, anyone investigating varieties of exile will come across numerous singular events, each one unique in some way. Clearly, the use of the word "exile" has caused, and continues to cause, different reactions in different people during different time periods. This is the inevitable starting point for such an investigation; when looking at so many diverse histories, what we first encounter are the differences. However, the experiences comprising these exiles are often connected to one another, as are the circumstances out of which they arise. Furthermore, very few experiences of any social significance can be reduced to nothing more than a one-time occurrence. For this reason, it is useful—even urgent—that our reflection abide by this first maxim:

> Strive to rid social phenomena of their own inner barriers and strive to do this again and again.

When confronted with an experience, we can better understand it if we rethink it in terms of a *type* of experience. Is this not the only way in which we are able to learn? Heeding these broad cues—that when adequately described, the experiences of exile, or any other social experience for that matter, are capable of extending beyond themselves and, by transcending their singularizing properties, it is possible through reflection to uncover certain common dimensions—I will attempt to rescue both direct and indirect lessons in exile.

To this end, in the first chapter "Words, Words, Words" I consider the specific uses of three words that are frequently used interchangeably in everyday speech: "exile," "refugee" and "emigrant." Upon closer examination, however, their nuances and contrasts become apparent. Concerning the first word, "exile," anyone undertaking any sort of historical research will sooner or later encounter vestiges of a wisdom that began to take shape in ancient times, for example, in the Bible as well as in Greece and Rome. We might then ask ourselves: Why have these lessons been all but lost in the modern era?

 | DOI:10.1163/9789004385153_002

Perhaps now is the right moment to consider this and various other questions concerning exile. Why? It is not difficult to confirm that the word "exile" is vanishing ever so gradually from our more habitual discourse (although it is unclear what might happen tomorrow). More and more we hear of human masses being displaced and, in many cases, even entire towns suffering hardship and neglect who are forced to do so. In such situations, what materials can we turn to in order to learn their potential lessons in exile?

Continuing with this gradual approach, in the second chapter "Testimonies and Metatestimonies" I examine how it is possible to recover such experiences. I will not refer to the most common types of testimonies, those more readily available such as life histories, memories, autobiographies, surveys or statistics, despite the risk that this act of partiality might pose to the integrity of the study. Instead, I will only consider atypical testimonies: poems which I will read as metatestimonies. Risking an even greater descent into this biased gaze, in the third chapter "Exile as Loss," the fourth chapter "Exile as Resistance" and the fifth chapter "Exile as a New Beginning" I limit myself among those possible metatestimonies to an examination of verses from two recent instances of exile: the Spanish exile that followed the fall of the Republic in the first half of the twentieth century and, in the second half, Latin America's Southern Cone exile. In those readings, we rediscover types of experiences (at least, this is what I am proposing) that have already been seen in Antiquity in some way or another, and that, as the chapter titles indicate, can be reconstructed through the beliefs, emotions and hopes of those subjected to exile, suffering through it as loss, transforming it into resistance or celebrating it as a new beginning.

Through these types of experiences, which also often overlap and tend to move between one type and another, we encounter the first class of lessons concerning how one should live such experiences of loss, resistance and new beginnings: *exile's direct lessons*. However, if we keep in mind the maxim of ridding social phenomena of their successive barriers, our investigative efforts lead us to other tasks of reflection.

Typically, when involved in an expedition, the thinking person aspires above all else to remain open to whatever the materials—scientific investigations or histories, alongside hopes, memories, songs—may render, which they gather little by little according to the topic of interest. Under these circumstances, digressions, ruptures and their consequences are welcome, including leaving behind loose ends, confronting unexpected difficulties or even deciding to look elsewhere.

I introduce one such rupture in the sixth chapter "Words Say, Words Resonate." Why? It is easy to demonstrate that even in very casual uses of the word "exile," its experiences "resonate"; innumerable metaphors are constantly being generated: "I find myself exiled from the sea ..." And not only that. By considering their particularities abstractly, certain types of exile experiences can shine a light into often-overlooked corners of human life, even making it possible for us to use those materials to develop new perspectives for our reflection.

For this reason, once again at the risk of partiality, I accept exile as both an *object of* learning and a *perspective for* learning. Thus, in the (perhaps needlessly) complex final chapter "Nomadic Cultures and Personhood," I reopen several excessively ambitious questions. Do not certain exile experiences make the case that culture as a whole should be redescribed as nomadic? Could it be that cultural identities do not in fact exist? And above all, what practical norms and morals can be upheld according to many of those experiences, and what notion of personhood? We can consider—at least I intend to consider—the answers to these questions on how adopting exile as a perspective makes it possible for us to redescribe cultures, morals and people in terms of a second category of reflective tasks: *exile's indirect lessons*. (We learn indirect lessons every day. In what is usually referred to as "the school of life," we experience both direct and indirect lessons.)

Caveat: This dense map is in no way a full account of the twists and turns that shape the path we plan to take. By consulting it, we can only vaguely anticipate the road that lies ahead.

CHAPTER 1

Words, Words, Words

Let me reiterate what we already know: Exile has given rise to different desires, beliefs, emotions and expectations in different societies during different historical periods and, presumably, has been accompanied by long-suffered acts of learning and unlearning. Even so, provided that fairly general lessons in exile do indeed exist, which individuals are capable of acquiring them? Is it only those who have suffered through these humiliating situations? During undoubtedly painful forms of learning and unlearning, are we not called upon to develop new approaches for conceiving certain articulations of communal life, such as those we refer to as "face-to-face interactions," "institutions," "citizenship rights," "foreign status," "the State" or "cosmopolitanism"? Do we not also face the task of rebuilding culture, the cement of our social structures, differently? Let us not get ahead of ourselves.

Most of all, let us not deny ourselves the option of taking our time and exploring alternative adjacent paths, those digressions that seem to be leading us away from our priorities when, in fact, they are helping us to reach them more effectively. Those heavily-trafficked routes of reflection, those that are fastest and most direct, can also sometimes rob us of what is important: that we alter little by little some of our deeply-rooted perspectives, that we be resolute in our effort to always be ready for an encounter with the unexpected.

Without concerning myself too much at this point with the fact that if I intend to rid the exile phenomenon of its frequently oppressive dead ends, I will have to first find my way through them, I consider it once again useful, at least for those just beginning their exploration, not to overlook a second maxim, often repeated yet seldom heeded: *Be careful with words!*

In this case, of course, I hope to initiate a rebuilding process around the words "lessons in exile." How so? I will focus my attention on the second term first, considering uses of the word "exile" and comparing those uses to other words with which it interacts in everyday life such as "refugee" or "emigrant." At the same time, I will use historical research to distinguish these words from one another.

To begin, anyone consulting a dictionary, even the most absent-minded of us, will find that exile is defined as a banishment imposed through political persecution.

Anyone looking a little deeper will then learn that "to banish" is understood as an action where:

 | DOI:10.1163/9789004385153_003

> as a form of punishment, those who govern use threats to indirectly force a person or group of people to leave their country. Or, by enacting criminal penalties, they directly expel a person or group of people from a certain territory.

When examining the uses of one word, we inevitably find our way to other words. Inside this expanding labyrinth, our reflection must make a choice with every step forward. For example, words like "exile" lead to words like "deported," "banished," "expatriated," "refugee" and "emigrant," but not to such enigmatic words as "ostracized," "transhumance" or "diaspora," or to unsettling words like "collective migrations." For some time now, many of these words have been shocking us every day in the mass media and now they have ceased to say anything at all. They only cause frustration. Let us turn our attention to two examples:

> *Refugee*: a word applied to people who, as a consequence of war and/or political persecution, must live in a country other than their own, often in poor conditions.

> *Emigrant*: a word applied to people who, for various types of reasons, have left their own country in order to establish themselves advantageously in another country.

What is the difference between an exile and a refugee? The uses of the word not only differ in the cognitive content they express, but also in the "color" or "colors" that permeate those discourses in which they participate. The quality that Frege referred to as "the color of words" or "the color of statements" can be restored by considering both implicit judgments of value as well as memories, emotions and the images that they tend to generate. Borges uses the expression "dialect of allusions" to describe this quality, or something akin to it, while some linguists refer to it less eloquently as "connotation." Although it is often not possible to distinguish a word's cognitive content from its color, let alone its evaluative force, sometimes attempting to do so can be advantageous, even if done using an artificial and labored abstraction. (For example, the expressions "that man" and "that creep" may reference the same individual but with differing appreciation. Also, words like "resolved" or "tenacious" express admiration when used to describe a person, whereas words like "inflexible," "obstinate" or "stubborn" express disapproval.)

Anyone not neglecting historical investigation when examining the dialects of allusions evoked by the words "exile" and "exiled" will come across a number of aphorisms, lamentations, consolations, hymns and reflections from the Bible as well as from Ancient Greece and Rome. In both cultural traditions, such circumstances are bestowed with vague dignity. I have no desire to reminisce about what was left behind and is no longer of any concern to us: let the past remain in the past. However, I try to be a better listener to those distant voices of the past that are still present, resonating inside us, albeit sometimes only intermittently. As we know, it can be helpful to sniff around a bit in the archives of a *present past*, including the dark corners of certain memories.

"Our Bones are Dried up"—"Build Houses and Dwell in Them"

Relying on diverse sources and no less diverse genres—historical books, prophesies, proverbs, aphorisms, parables, imaginations—the Bible narrates stories that are simultaneously interpreted as lessons: how humanity loses sight of and then rediscovers justice and God. It is not surprising that an experience as agonizing as the Babylonian exile gave rise to words that continue to question why so much evil occurred and what we can reveal by taking this suffering into account. But what happened?

Following the death of the reformer King Josiah in the year 609 BCE, the Kingdom of Judah began its decline, eventually falling to Egyptian rule. In 605 BCE, the Babylonian army, under the command of Nebuchadnezzar, defeated the Egyptians and laid siege to Jerusalem. In 597 BCE Jerusalem surrendered, and many Jews were forced to set out for Babylonia. Almost immediately, the outward displays of protest found in many of the Bible's books are replaced by a desire for self-examination, that is, a withdrawal inward. Both the prophets and historical books blame Israel for its own misfortune. This first exile is not experienced as an arbitrary act of fate, but as a punishment that was to be expected. For this reason, in order to eliminate the cause of suffering we must again identify precisely what part of the blame one bears. Otherwise, the rest of one's days will be poisoned. (It takes courage to resist confusing misfortune with a plan or dream that fails as a result of one's own vices or errors.) In 2 Kings, 21:11 we read:

> Because Manasseh king of Judah has done these abominations (he has acted more wickedly than all the Amorites who were before him and has also made Judah sin with his idols), therefore thus says the Lord God of Israel: "Behold, I am bringing such calamity upon Jerusalem and Judah, that whoever hears of it, both his ears will tingle."

Similar passages continue to appear, for instance, in 1 Kings 11:4–13; 2 Kings 23:31–25, 30; 2 Chronicles 36, etc. Unfortunately, the situation continued to worsen. In the year 588 BCE, after several plans for a rebellion, Jerusalem refused to send its tribute to Babylonia. Nebuchadnezzar then launched a new siege, and on August 17, 586 BCE Jerusalem and its temples were destroyed. This second exile unleashed panic among those who had remained in Jerusalem under the impression that they were now safe. These panics have not been uncommon in exilic histories. Oftentimes, a segment of the population that stays home projects the blame for their misfortune upon those who were forced to leave. Then, once the guilty party is in exile, a false sense of confidence is recovered, which is again shattered suddenly and without explanation (Jeremiah 24; Ezekiel 11:14–21). And still a third exile is briefly suggested in 582 BCE (Jeremiah 52:30).

Throughout this period, the torturous sense of loss and desolation grows increasingly more profound: "our bones are dried up … we are completely destroyed" (Ezekiel 37:11). At the same time, however, the prophets underline the need to gather strength in order to distance oneself from those two wicked accomplices that every one of us tends to invite along and that seduce us by feeding off our hardships: enthusiastic but empty words and desires that get lost in the corridors, unraveling inside fantasy.

It is also vital that we not let ourselves become paralyzed by that third accomplice: incessant rage. (Unfortunately, it is often difficult to realize early enough that we are in poor company.) For this reason, it is worth citing a passage from Jeremiah's letter in which he calls upon the exiled not to neglect the most effective weapon available to them during a state of exile or any other misfortune: countering the overwhelming emotions and desires provoked by such an event with one's own imagination, plans and an iron will to immediately set about making them a reality.

> Build houses and dwell in them, plant orchards and eat of their fruit. Take wives and have sons and daughters; take wives for your sons, and give your daughters in marriage, that they may bear sons and daughters; multiply there and do not decrease. But seek the welfare of the city where I have sent you into exile, and pray to the LORD on its behalf, for in its welfare you will find your welfare. (Jeremiah 29:5-7)

Ezekiel is a typical prophet of exile. His life is often even presented as an allegory for exile. Ezekiel was banished to Babylon where he strongly denounced the betrayal of Israel, thus reinforcing his prophesy of the fall of Jerusalem.

He unexpectedly loses his wife and is left temporarily mute, which is interpreted to be the silence of God amid catastrophe (Ezekiel 3:26–27, 24:25–27, 33:21–22). In a second phase Ezekiel, having recovered his voice, becomes that sentinel (33:21–22) whose exhortations—his concentration charged with lucidity and inspiration—not only help him to resist but also pave the way for a possible future. One quality of the Book of Ezekiel, written as a rough autobiography, is its emphasis on the need to look beyond the appearances of things. It states that by attributing befallen evils to the errors of one's ancestors or the community, one has already begun heading down the wrong path (Ezekiel 14:12–23, 18, 33:10–20). Simply by assuming responsibility, a heavy yet inalienable burden, one can break from what are sometimes contrived to be the chains of misfortune: obstacles that are still paralyzing despite being the products of deceptive desperation and fear.

There is perhaps an even more exemplary prophet of exile, a strange voice discernible in passing in certain hidden corners of the Book of Isaiah (40–55). Since the end of the eighteenth century, the Book of Isaiah has been attributed to a figure referred to as "Deutero-Isaiah." The characteristically desolate atmosphere of biblical exile changes with the book's very first words: "Comfort, comfort my people" (40:1). One ceases to scrutinize their own guilt and instead searches to break with the past in order to encourage the recovery needed to again be capable of happiness.

> Every valley shall be exalted, and every mountain and hill brought low;
> And the rough ground shall be transformed into plain and hills into fertile lowland. (40:4)

These canticles encourage trusting in the power of the word—"Jehovah has given me the tongue of disciples that I may know how to nourish the weary with the word" (50:4)—as a way to bolster the arduous task of healing the injuries of exile (a task that is arduous because, among other reasons, it is usually undesirable and even actively discouraging). But what is most astonishing of all, joyously astonishing, is the universalism of Deutero-Isaiah's voice. At times, it even seems to be a precursor to Stoic cosmopolitanism. It speaks "to the nations" and describes the differences separating them as being inconsequential. Isaiah 41:1 urges:

> Let the peoples renew their strength.
> Let them approach, then let them speak; let us together draw near for judgment!

However, the diverse lessons in these exiles are not realized by following a more or less straight path. There is an ebb and flow between incapacitating desolation and the will to begin anew. It is clear that in some of the Bible's poetic books, such as Lamentations (except maybe for the third and most universal one), there is a return to earlier emotions, those imposed upon almost every subsequent exile and consistent with the initial experience of exile: exile as overwhelming loss. Powerful feelings of melancholy and mourning also circulate throughout some of the Psalms, e.g., 137 and 74: "Remember your community, which you acquired long ago; [...] the dark corners of the nation are full of the haunts of violence." Contrarily, other Psalms alluding to experiences after exile—e.g., 85 ("righteousness and peace have embraced one another") or 126 ("they who sow with tears will reap with songs of joy")—trace the outline of a door that is opening or that is already open.

I will now, not without a certain amount of impatience, move on to another grand assembly of words relative to ancient exile. While these reflections describe the same experiences in Greece and Rome, they are often very different from those collected in the Bible. *Caveat*: Although mostly buried, there are still lingering vestiges of both classes of wisdom; they constitute a *present past*. (For such wisdom to take effect, it often only requires the right occasion, similar to fertilizer strewn across the ground.)

"I Am a Foreigner in Every Land"—"In Every Land I Am at Home"

According to *Lives and Opinions of Eminent Philosophers* by Diogenes Laërtius—an essential text because of its many insights into Greek thought, its modest gossip and revered stories—the first treatise devoted to, among other things, a moral discussion of the theme of exile appears to have been a dialogue by Aristippus entitled *To the Exiles*. (Incredibly, a popular Spanish edition "translates" it as *To the Fugitives*. Another symptom: when listing Aristippus' publications, Laërtius placed it immediately after the dialogue *To the Shipwrecked* and before *To a Beggar*.) Who was this Aristippus?

Born in Cyrene in 435 BCE (and dying in 355 BCE, also in Cyrene), Aristippus arrived in Athens like so many others, drawn to Socrates' fame. He was partly responsible for a new tradition of schools that can be grouped under the category of "alternative Socratism." This Socratism was often seen as scandalous when compared with Plato or Aristotle's "institutional Socratism" (or more accurately, "contrafactively institutional Socratism"), devoted as they were to the idea of the *polis* and, thus, to the contemplation of the structures and laws in a well-ordered society, when they were not proposing partial, or even radical, institutional reconstructions. But, why do I preserve the word "Socratism" in relation to both traditions despite the enduring opposition between them?

Like other adherents of alternative Socratism, Socrates made—not without some arrogance—a vocation out of the practice of public offense: he was hated by both the democratic and oligarchic parties intermittently. (For example: he infuriated the democrats by voting against holding a common trial for generals who had not buried the dead after the Battle of Arginusae. However, he equally infuriated the oligarchs by refusing to approve the arrest of Leon of Salamis.) Worse still, if we reread Plato's first "Socratic" dialogues as being more or less faithful reports of Socrates' conduct, we find that what tradition has incessantly praised as "fine Socratic irony" is merely crude, audacious insolence that knows no restraint where a value of importance is concerned, regardless of the status of his interlocutor. He makes no exceptions for disciples or friends, including those such as Alcibiades who declare their love for him. Given this absence of filter or even any basic sense of discretion and courtesy, it is not surprising that sooner or later accusations of impiety and corrupting the youth would be formulated against Socrates, ultimately leading to his death sentence, though he was found guilty by only a few votes.

However, acting in accordance with what his conscience recognizes as a value, e.g., truth, does not prevent Socrates from simultaneously benefitting from an institutional—even traditionally institutional—form of Socratism. I would almost say—not without a certain element of paradox—that Socrates defends the obligation to obey the laws and decisions of the *polis*, even if he judges them to be unjust. In the *Crito* dialogue, when Socrates' friends are informed that he has been condemned to death, they beg him to go into exile. (Considering the ease with which he is granted the possibility of escape, the reader gets the feeling that all of Athens is begging him to flee.) Nevertheless, Socrates adopts an institutional Socratism like none other, declaring that as a good citizen he will not violate the laws of the *polis* under any circumstances, least of all on this frighteningly important occasion. (Plato and Aristotle are not quite as respectful towards institutions and accept exile as a lesser evil.)

Let us now turn our attention to Aristippus and alternative Socratism. Like nearly all Greeks, Aristippus considers happiness to be the purpose of life, and in order to achieve it one must possess self-control. This is only gained by practicing a dual resistance: one must learn to resist immediate urges, such as those of the body or those arising out of habit, while also resisting the obligations imposed by social identifications and counteridentifications. Once this self-control is reached, one may feel free to enjoy the many intense pleasures of the world and even the obligations that are part and parcel of social coexistence, without fear of enslavement. When do we let ourselves be enslaved? Who is a slave? Aristippus' response: "He who is free to leave is not a slave." The ability to distance oneself from one's own impulses and from any city (today we would say from any country, from any nation); therein lies the key. This is why for Aristippus, only those who do not fear exile, even provoking it, can truly understand what freedom is. In a poignant, oft-quoted discussion that Xenophon inserts in the *Memorabilia*, Aristippus, in opposition to the institutional Socratism of his venerated teacher, declares: "I am not subservient to any State. I am a foreigner in every land."

This way of understanding exile's lessons, the pinnacle of otherness as one assumes the role of the perennial foreigner, becomes radicalized later by one of Ancient Greece's schools of thought, one which still to this day draws malice and rapt fury; their self-imposed name "Cynics" literally suggests acting "like dogs." (The modern use of the word "cynical" is a caricature that was perhaps cultivated by the inheritors of "institutional Socratism.") In the expression "human animal," the Cynics attempt to recover what has been stolen from us: the word "animal." In this way, they manage to "falsify the coinage" that has left this animal so hopeless, to take a step backwards when faced with the subjugation born of "passions," of "participation in political activities," of "fame," of the "acquisition of riches," of "power." (Centuries later, in an act of inheriting while carefully innovating—a task so difficult to sustain yet so productive when one is capable of it—Nietzsche revisits the cynical expression "defacing the currency" and makes it his anthem: the "inversion of values.") Through this "defacing of currency," whereby the meanings of accepted values are reassigned, the ancient Cynic acquires the strength to resist temptations and strokes of good fortune. How? By living simply (drinking water, eating frugally, choosing the hard floor as their bed) and by heeding the voices of two sagacious advisors: exile and bad reputation. (In order not to incur the latter, one should not deny oneself such actions as masturbation, public copulation or socializing with prostitutes.) Once again, we see that some falls can also be potential tools for ascent or methods towards decipherment and resurgence (or, at least they can be used as such given the right amount of clarity). How does this work?

Few social relationships seem to be as "natural" as systems of belonging, for example, belonging by birthright to a particular family, a culture, a nation or a State. However, there are few social constructions like these forms of belonging that so violently conceal the fact that they were, and continue to be, the result of cruel lengthy battles also carried out inside each and every person. Once established, each form of belonging provides shelter—a shelter made of protection, recognition, comforts and even privileges—while simultaneously imposing often excessive obligations. Such services of protection regularly involve humiliating servitude and even compromises that in extreme situations can result in death. This is why we must mind the Cynics when they advise us to never lose sight of the fact that those systems of belonging do not emerge from the natural world. They only exist because some human animals have invented them (i.e., articulated them, established them, defended them ...). Diogenes Laërtius recounts that when Diogenes the Cynic was asked what advantage could come from reflection, his response was similar to one that Aristippus might have given: "The advantage of being prepared for any eventuality." This explains the long staff these provocative thinkers carried with them as part of their practice in remaining constantly ready to abandon their jobs, their places of residency, their plans and even their passions.

Unsurprisingly, the Cynics also invented a word that sounds like a terrible oxymoron to the ears of institutional Socratism and of course to those of our own political tradition derived from it: we must insist on exploring the many landscapes, the many cities, and listening to their incessant rumbling as they modernize so that we might become "cosmopolitans." For this is the goal: to be "citizens of the world."

It is generally agreed upon that Aristippus and the Cynics' loud negative cosmopolitanism finds its successor in the positive cosmopolitanism of the well-mannered Stoics, who are complicated inheritors nonetheless considering their general discomfort with such an inheritance. The Stoic motto could be: "I am not subservient to any State. I am at home everywhere."

Caveat: During this time in Rome, Stoicism was not the only way of responding to exile. Ovid notoriously shaped exile into a representation of absolute desolation, reminiscent of the Book of Lamentations and of several of the Psalms. However, unlike these biblical texts, at no moment does he present it as a justifiable punishment. Without minimizing the shadowy pathos of both *Tristia* and *Epistulae ex Ponto*, Ovid never ceases his lament. He even describes the distance forced between him and his beloved landscapes as the cruelest of hells. All he has left are his words, full of nostalgia and protest, to escape the circumstances imposed upon him. In *Tristia V* he confesses:

> So, I drag out my life and time, and I attempt retreat from myself and banish the contemplation of my troubles.

What is at the root of such sorrow? Maybe we are no longer able to grasp the suffering found in the Bible, nor the uproar caused by alternative Socratism (Aristippus, the Cynics and, to a certain extent, the Stoics) and its defiant use of words like "exile" and "foreigner," nor the grief expressed in Ovid's exilic verses.

If we wish to recover that immeasurable pain and fear, we must also consider the value that the idea of *place* held in those communities that had recently developed sedentary traditions in Antiquity, including Greece and Rome.

Let us not forget, one's *place* of residency was the land of ancestors. After their death, past generations continued to live beneath the ground, receiving ritual foods for example. The sacred sphere in which religious rituals were carried out was therefore synonymous with the subterranean space occupied by those of the same blood who had preceded them on earth. This is why it was a desecration for anyone not belonging to the family to participate in these rituals. Even much later, when an array of common gods emerged in the ancient cities, public religion did not supplant the private rituals that continued to unite families. In fact, to a certain extent public religion inherited the exclusionary character of those rituals: part of being a member of a community, and even of enjoying the rights available to a citizen, included worshipping the same gods.

As a result, among many other consequences, foreigners in Greece and Rome—that is, individuals who were not protected by the gods of the city in which they were living—could not acquire property because land (*place*) was another component of one's genealogy. With this in mind, despite the fact that those thinkers grouped together under alternative Socratism had transformed exile into a sagacious advisor, we should not forget that in Rome exile was juridically considered to be capital punishment. Foreigners had no hope of becoming citizens of other lands or ever receiving protection from other gods.

Caveat: Let us not be complicit in covering those precious remaining footprints of lessons which still exist despite so many efforts to trample them and erase them forever. Alternative Socratism's praise of exile, while rarely evoked in social life, endured as a corrosive proposition in thought that has been revisited every so often. In the same Rome, little more than a generation after Ovid, Seneca once again breaks with the moral tradition of experiencing exile as loss or condemnation. In his own way, Seneca defends the legacy of alternative Socratism through the Stoics' more respectable version. Exile is not evil. Since every individual is a citizen of the world, the homeland can be found everywhere. One can live in Corsica just as in Rome. It is possible with each step to disregard a wall, a customs house, breathe deeply and continue marching onward.

When Seneca was exiled by the emperor Claudius from 41 to 49 CE, he consolingly wrote to his mother that exile cannot take from us anything of too great importance since it cannot steal "nature, which is universal, and virtue, which is ours." Centuries later in a very different theoretical context but still riddled with overtly Stoic echoes, Kant appears to paraphrase that same far-reaching and illuminating affirmation in *Groundwork of the Metaphysics of Morals*. It would perhaps be worthwhile to reexamine this entire treatise, considered with good reason to be one of the most influential in moral theory of modern times, but through a foreign lens; to read it as if it had been written by an exile contemplating their condition.

At this point I must abruptly wrap up this very brief tour of the diverse colors that Antiquity's discourses and practices have infused into the circumstances of exile. Nevertheless, in these few historical odds and ends, have we not already discovered certain direct lessons in exile, or at least, traces of them?

Demands from Different Directions

Now I want to address the condition—perhaps too dismal in color—referred to by the word "refugee." As far as this condition is concerned, we will find no support in the illustrious schools of Greek thought alternating between their celebrations that "everyone is a foreigner in every land" and "everyone is at home in every land." Nor can we appeal to the keen observations of Dante, Madame de Stael or Joyce who consecrate—the religious color of this verb is appropriate—whoever goes into exile as a guardian of memory.

On the contrary, the moment the word "refugee" forces its way into the conversation, the topics quickly degenerate into questions of army and border patrols. All the devastating pain and misery of displacement is only multiplied inside the dialects of allusions that encompass the word "refugee," as is one of its consequences: the very uninspiring regulations developed by "Departments of International Protection" and "United Nations High Commissioners." In such policies we learn about "access to asylum procedures," "the willingness of the State to admit refugees," "visa denial," "denied border entry," "restrictive asylum practices in accordance with the petitioner's origin," "refugee stipulations when in large-scale numbers," "illegal entry," "causes for expulsion," "irregular movements of refugees," "sexual violence against women and children," "torture," etc. What else must we add to the list to further confirm this "often bad" way of life alluded to in the characterization suggested by the word "refugee"?

Let us imagine that we are among that group of (perhaps naïve) people who are still not resigned to idea that "reality"—a coarse and ordinary word—is nothing more than a collection of mere spectacles staged upon words, images and sounds by mass media or by the System, by Rhetoric or by something else of that nature. Then we will surely believe that, along with these social constructions, there "really" (to continue insisting on this adverb, which is no less ordinary than the adjective from which it comes) are people, such as refugees, who "really" find themselves on the brink of death due to hunger and cold, and who are cheated by "human traffickers" or "polleros," as they are called in Mexico. What is more, those unfortunate people are often tortured or raped when they attempt to cross a border, or they drown when a boat cannot hold them all or die in armed attacks against the settlements where they have been crowded together like cattle.

Let us not allow ourselves to be paralyzed by the horror. Let us also consider words like "migrate" and "emigrant." Compared to the other words that we have been associating and differentiating, these are the ones whose uses are on the rise. Human migrations have even been equated with animal behavior. (It is common to consider such movements as one of the various evolutionary forces, along with natural selection, genetic drift and mutations.) However, I want to avoid any considerations having to do with population genetics. Even if we limit ourselves to the modern, international concept of "emigrant," its content remains ambiguous: An "emigrant" is one who has left their homeland in order to establish themself in another country either because they have obtained employment or out of a desire for adventure. An "emigrant" is also one who is part of a vast displacement of people for economic, political and religious reasons. Among the motives for emigrating we will find "reasons that entice" or those incentives that encourage one to abandon their home country. Also cited are "reasons that drive," for example, statements like "hunger drives one to desperation" or "hunger will drive one to do anything." What is currently "driving" people to emigrate are lack of employment, political despotism and misery. In these last cases, we once again encounter forced actions, such as exile.

Of course, our reflection on the usage of these three words—"exile," "refugee" and "emigrant"—could continue gathering historical, anthropological and juridical information from a number of directions. (Each one of these directions unsurprisingly carries its own significant problems which have given rise to many investigations.) However, regardless of their differences, being careful with the words "exile," "refugee" and, if not with all the uses of the word "emigrant," then at least with a large number of them, will help us not to forget that we are facing a single category of actions: those made during forced displacements. (In relation to these types of actions, we must not overlook the fact that the adjective "forced" is applied in each situation for different reasons. Let us also not forget that one situation can easily become any one of the others.)

Nevertheless, we must now make certain clarifications regarding these three words. If we arrange their painful experiences, even only loosely, in such a way as to determine varying degrees of pain, then within exiles we will find (if I may use these murky and possibly even callous-sounding words) "moderate degrees." In general, exile has been suffered and continues to be suffered as an experience that brings about serious pain, just as with any other action carried out against one's will. But in modern times this pain is considerably less than that stemming from torture, imprisonment, murder or, even worse, death camps.

Additionally, there are multiple perspectives for approaching this suffering and each involves its own set of demands. With forced displacements, we often assume certain perspectives that lead to the demands of one's subjectivity and its experiences. In the case of exiles, it is about managing their fears, anxieties, desires, fantasies, guilt, expectations, obligations, hopes and consolations. Indeed, there is ample material for us to consider in the Bible and in the traditions of alternative Socratism vis-à-vis this perspective.

There are also other possible perspectives, for example, those which face the opposite direction toward the sociological, anthropological and administrative demands related to social circumstances or "objective factors" and, consequently, the politics of displaced masses. These types of investigations will need to consider official documents from national states or the United Nations and from NGOs that work with exiles, refugees and immigrants, both documented and undocumented.

I am not suggesting anything absurd, such as that subjectivity and its psychological and normative tensions have little to do with social life, the State or politics. Nor am I suggesting the counter-absurdity, which would be no less intolerable: that we should not examine subjective problems when discussing the issue of displaced masses. Each subjectivity represents a thread in a web of social relations—political, legal, economic, cultural—constructed between national societies and state and market institutions. At the same time, those societies, traditions and institutions are formed—and every day they are either reaffirmed or eroded—as a result of the cooperation and confrontations between these diverse subjectivities.

However, despite their interrelations, if on the one hand, one looks at the aggressive behavior of an exiled adolescent, the misfortune of a war widow or the almost imperceptible protests of an elderly person living in an overcrowded refugee colony, and on the other, the juridical orders and budgets of a particular State receiving asylum requests, are the demands and our ways of satisfying them so radically different?

I Present Certain Propositions to Instill Order in the Detours Taken throughout this Reflection, (and, at the Same Time, I Leave behind Various Loose Ends that Will Later Grant Access to Exile's Indirect Lessons)

The *first proposition* confirms a forgetfulness, a stubborn forgetfulness: *anyone turning to the norms, consolations, ingenuity and arguments put forth in the Bible, alternative Socratism and Greece and Rome to satisfy the demands of their subjectivity (regarding how exile should be experienced and, thus, how to gain access to exile's direct lessons), will easily recognize an interruption of that wisdom in the modern era, at least in the sense of a relatively systematic moral reflection.*

In the best of cases, this wisdom was replaced with (usually descriptive) investigations from the social sciences or with discussions on the regulations of international organizations and during bad times, with a trivializing moralism (if I may again use a reasonable pleonasm). But perhaps "trivializing moralism" falls short and we should use the word "caricature," or more to the point: "nonsense." This is no exaggeration. Read for example the *Familiar Epistles* by Sir Antonio de Guevara (1539–1541), in particular the one that opens with the epigraph "Letter for Don Pedro Girón when he was banished to Oran. A very remarkable letter for all men who are banished and grief-stricken." De Guevara, who is more eager to comply with the norms of courtier discourse than to do justice to the demands imposed by exile, imitates Plutarch's illustrious *On Exile*, even borrowing (at times erroneous) historical examples from him. Let us not mince words: despite his philanthropic influence on so many statespeople and lawyers, and on tradition in general, there is a certain contagious moralism already present in Plutarch himself. His famous work, with its admirable passages, reveals an eclectic reception of Cynic, Stoic and even Platonic arguments in a tone that at times borders on cloying.

Disregarding even more—much more—the fact that exile belongs to a class of forced displacements, De Guevara redescribes exile as a situation with only privileges to offer: nobody envies the banished individual or asks them for money; they have no need to spend on appearances or on servants; "they are not obligated to maintain a house or to dwell with their spouse"; they can write and engage in all varieties of falsehoods; they do not have to pay tributes or "celebrate, host, feast, rejoice." (Is one who finds themself in exile not merely a grand tourist under slightly imposed conditions? De Guevara also argues that "all free men desire to enjoy" such "privileges," though this enthusiasm is completely unrelated to that of the Cynics despite his use of apparently similar words).

All the same, in addition to allowing us to recall these trivialities, the first proposition also invites us to explore other, unexpected directions. Gathering materials that will broaden the horizon that surrounds exile, I expand on them in a way that is perhaps odd and, at least at first glance, must seem excessively hospitable to chaos. For the time being, might we be able to draw a parallel between the interruption in modern history of this wisdom regarding exile and the decline in the Middle Ages of reflections on friendship, which dominated the discourse of the ancients? Still, what relationships can be restored between such disparate situations, at least on the surface, as exile and friendship? Furthermore, what could possibly connect these two historical declines which initially appear to be completely unrelated?

Let us refer also to the *Déclaration des droits de l'homme et du citoyen* from 1789. Is this detour too disconcerting? In response to the vigorous nonconformity of many women, the word "*homme*" in this declaration has been subsequently translated/interpreted as "person." If revolutionary France's *Déclaration* is translated/interpreted as "Declaration of the Rights of the Person and of the Citizen," then are the rights of persons equated with rights of citizenship? Such an identification is useful in determining the actual content of these rights since they clearly acquire somewhat precise meanings in terms of a particular State's legal and political rights. In addition to these rights, however, when persons are being identified and counteridentified, consideration is also given to the economic attributes of a particular market. But I wonder whether personhood can be defined solely according to State and market attributes while omitting, for example, the demands of subjectivity? Are there not persons existing outside of these predetermined limits decided on by a State or market? Individuals forced into exile would seemingly have lost a significant amount, or perhaps all, of their legal and political rights as well as much or perhaps all of their economic potential. Until they are able to obtain new citizenship, they will continue to be without the legal and political rights of another State. Does this mean they have ceased to be persons?

From these complex anxieties, I now present a *second proposition*, another (perhaps even more surprising) detour in this argumentation in which we move from exile as an object of learning to exile as a perspective for learning: *if exile is adopted as a perspective, sooner or later we will likely find ourselves faced with the following dilemma, or apparent dilemma, concerning personhood: personhood is either reduced to certain social concepts (for example, certain legal and political rights and certain economic attributes), or personhood is independent of these concepts.*

Though disorienting at times, these detours, and with them the accumulation of materials pulling us in different directions, are rarely useless when beginning an exploration. With this in mind, I will hold onto my explanation of this second proposition for now, which we will take up again, more deliberately, in the final chapter as part of exile's *indirect* lessons.

Let us refocus our attention. For anyone accepting the first option in this dilemma, the word "person" refers to nothing more than a decorative figure intended to confuse us with humanistic rhetoric. After all, only people are identified in many social concepts: political and legal concepts like "citizenship," or economic concepts such as individuals belonging to groups with certain levels of income and purchasing power. Perhaps we should remember that traditional societies were designed by promoting diverse modes of conduct that instilled a certain amount of order to existence. In many of them, the duties of citizenship, or some relatively equivalent idea, required that each adult male fulfill the obligations designated by his social position. (Foreigners were excluded from these tasks, as were, to a large extent, those semi-foreigners who from a political, legal and often economic perspective have, until very recently, been women.) We might also add here that we should be careful not to get too carried away with such a vague expression as "traditional societies." What has been stated about such societies, with relevant adjustments for each time period and their particular circumstances, is generally valid. Does not every society organize itself as a system of belonging produced by its various social positions, which in turn produces those very same positions? For example, legal institutions produce and are produced through the positions of "legislator," "prosecutor," "attorney," "police officer," "criminal" and "victim," among others. Part of the process of social stability is realized through the fulfillment of rules that govern actions as well as desires, beliefs and emotions, which suggests that a social position is reinforced by what is socially expected. Therefore, if we have information about what it means to act like a judge, attorney or police officer, we can predict a significant amount of their actions, along with their desires, beliefs and emotions, regardless of the history of the unique individual who accepts such a position. It will no doubt be noted here that personhood is not only being descriptively reduced to a group of predetermined behavior patterns, but also that from those patterns it is being normatively reduced according to the degree to which those expectations are fulfilled. In this way, we use such expressions as "the functional (or dysfunctional) behavior of a judge, attorney, police officer, etc. within the social system."

In support of the dilemma's first option, one could look to Burke's antihumanist cry (or possibly "anti-person," if by "person" we mean a concept that cannot be reduced to its social determinants). He favored his very practical and well-defined rights as an English citizen to his intangible rights as a person, that is, his "human rights" (perhaps the only rights that exiles and refugees can hope for). His cry is indicative of a certain tendency that has since been reinforced: what matters most is that we assume the political role of "citizen of a State" and nowadays, possess an identification card or passport. These "paper identities" are the only ones capable of guaranteeing protection. Such observations may explain, at least in part, the discontinuity in modern society's knowledge—indicated in the first proposition I presented—that is, an interruption within a more or less systematic moral reflection that focuses on those who, existing liminally to the social system, do not possess a paper identity; for example, those in exile.

However, let us assume that an exiled individual already possesses certain rights. Is it possible to confirm this? Under numerous political regimes these individuals cannot be sold, nor can they be tortured without retribution. At many borders, those who have fled in exile cannot be pursued unlike other species of animals that can unfortunately still be hunted. If there are limits to the mistreatment of these human animals, then presumably they possess certain rights. And since they possess them, these rights cannot be reduced to those acquired by belonging to the State, given that these individuals have been disowned by their State of origin and are not yet citizens of another. Personhood would therefore gain a certain descriptive, but first of all normative, independence from the political and legal concepts of citizenship as well as from any analogous economic concepts.

To defend the dilemma's second option concerning personhood, one might turn, or return, to the energy of alternative Socratism and its provocative cosmopolitan initiatives. What if we were to eliminate any dependence upon a State or market, that quality besetting political, legal and economic concepts, and establish in its place a corresponding cosmopolitanism in the amplest sense of the word? Consequently, how then might these attributes serve as determinants for personhood? I ask for a little more of your patience; rather than immediately extracting the content from several of exile's *direct* lessons, for now I will continue accumulating diverse materials.

Reasons for and against Certain Cosmopolitanisms

If we were to introduce a legal or political cosmopolitanism, then the legal or political limitations implied by the existence of a specific citizenship would be eliminated. Political cosmopolitanism, for example, rejects all nationalist arguments—or communitarian and multi-communitarian arguments in general—which uphold that all rights and political obligations depend upon the shared history or institutions within a group. Political cosmopolitanism does not recognize civil liberties—freedom of speech, freedom of movement, freedom of the press—or norms regarding the treatment of women, homosexuals or the disabled as contingent upon state laws or their uses and customs within a tradition. According to such cosmopolitanisms, rights and obligations, both political and legal, are exclusively valued as the rights and obligations of persons. In this case, does the condition of exile disappear?

Similarly, economic cosmopolitanism rejects that principles of distributive justice be applied to only one society, as this would presume a State's demarcation of the other societies to which those principles would not be applied. Economic cosmopolitanism requires that when exercising distributive justice, the borders between States must not be taken into consideration. For this reason, the principles of distributive justice should instead be applied directly to persons, independent of all legal or political tariffs.

Of course, despite their possible inconsistencies, the Stoic conviction that we are "citizens of the world" runs throughout these various cosmopolitanisms: "we are at home" in any geographical corner. But, how convincing is this argument from those who exclusively defend the second option in our dilemma? Do the experiences and possible lessons in exile play a role here?

One might perhaps object, arguing that this offers a delusional resolution to our dilemma regarding personhood—or, more politely, a theoretical resolution but not a practical one. In truth, we live and, as a result, we identify and individualize ourselves based on where we live. Additionally, even if it were possible to put such cosmopolitanisms into practice, there seem to be credible reasons to reject them, at least in their radical formulations.

For example, one might also say that a political or legal cosmopolitanism will require, between one *place* and another *place*, institutions and certain regulations in order to reinforce them, including systems of punishment. What guarantee do we have that "cosmopolitan institutions" will not become instruments of general despotism—a powerful, planetary-scale Leviathan more difficult to contain (and to defeat) than the localized leviathans we have known up until now? When used in politics, the local "here" is also a *place* of invaluable resistance and of social innovation. The insolence of the Cynics and their banner, their "I am a foreigner in every land," is precisely that: a challenge. It is, through its own characteristics, a civil transgression that assails, defies and inspires, but not out of any political program that it might accomplish, or even want to accomplish, just like many subsequent protests whose intention was primarily to disrupt (and which often unintentionally bear echoes of Aristippus, Diogenes the Cynic, Sappho, Bruno, Sor Juana, Thoreau ...).

Similar objections can be raised against a radical economic cosmopolitanism. When considering a market free of local restrictions, or its development based on a globalization of profit patterns, are we not running the risk of neglecting and even repressing the needs of different regions, namely of those *places* that are the least favored? Some of these needs frequently interfere with, or jeopardize, global productivity. But is this reason enough to eliminate them?

Caveat: Let us not give in so easily or, as an excuse, allow our resignation to once again raise walls around *each and every one of those places*. It is certainly possible to design legal, political and economic proposals through general and local dialectics, that is, through a world horizon that does not flatten out its many contours. These dialectics will have to uphold many cosmopolitan initiatives as well as one inescapable truth: we live where we live. I wonder: in order to refine such dialectics, can we gain anything by reflecting on exile? How? And why?

On one hand, with exile we encounter painful experiences that are moderate in degree, relatively rare compared to other forced displacements and which seem more and more to be a thing of the past (if we can say such a thing). And as we know, when thought can achieve focus and distance at the same time, it becomes more intense. Also, these are experiences that have received considerable attention, as we pointed out with respect to the Bible and alternative Socratism. By concentrating on exile among the list of many types of forced displacements, we facilitate the retrieval of inherited reflections from various *present pasts*.

On the other hand, no one will deny that forced displacements, the relevant category of actions to which exile belongs, have been a frequent plague throughout history. Even now these displacements have continued to multiply and the injustices and repeated misfortunes they trigger have increased. Furthermore, those who are displaced from their land have been made into defenseless figures and often an inconvenience because now they are impossible for us to overlook. For this reason, exploring some of the demands of subjectivity in exile—that is, without getting caught up in the *pars pro toto* fallacy, exploring what and how that *part* of a suffering subjectivity can teach us—can aid any investigation into the subjective demands of other varieties of forced displacements. Given the unfortunate pervasiveness of these events, perhaps this offers a unique method for tracking down fragments of self-construction that are common to all human animals. Moreover, is it not urgent that we regain the wisdom vis-à-vis exile elaborated in the Bible and alternative Socratism, which, according to the first proposition that I presented, has been disregarded throughout modern history? Supposing that several of these observations were true, where should we continue searching for exile's direct and indirect lessons?

CHAPTER 2

Testimonies and Metatestimonies

Trust is a natural sentiment for the human animal. We assume it to be something inherent, not acquired, and as having countless correlates both practical and theoretical, concrete and abstract. Unfortunately, trust can often waver. For good and bad reasons, we can begin to distrust all sorts of knowledge, including the words of others. We can also discover reasons to distrust ourselves. Forced displacements, for example, immediately produce distrust as well as other injuries. Contexts are then generated in which it is at times more, and at times less, reasonable for us to trust or distrust. This gives rise to *particular trust*: we trust certain groups and not others. It also encourages *singular trust*: under certain circumstances only a specific individual merits trust. Still, the reasons that once determined such particular and singular trust are regularly forgotten and spaces of general trust are reestablished. However, anxiety—the anxiety of exile, for example—is not forgotten. Necessarily, we continue trusting that countries will not disappear as soon as we leave them, that our new neighbors are not robots or that the milk we are buying in this shop that we are visiting for the first time has not been poisoned.

Nevertheless, alongside this general trust there is undoubtedly, somewhere in the shadows, a *principle of presumed trust* in operation, inherited from previously suffered anxieties. A presumption is a rule of action that expresses expectations regarding the future as well as the possibility of moderating these expectations according to each case and because of particular or singular reasons. For example, we trust certain knowledge from experience until we realize it to be not only a unique and unrepeatable experience, but also in conflict with other knowledge. Or, we trust certain words in a testimony until discovering particular or singular reasons against it. With some uproar, one might object: is this not an acceptance of traditionalism's blindness and even a naively confident attitude that transforms what "seems to me" or what "we feel" into criteria for truth? Not at all. A *principle of presumed trust* is not a *principle of general credulity*, which eliminates any room for debate by suggesting that a person should trust, for example, that seemingly truthful testimonies are objectively so. But how do these observations help us investigate the exile experience and, most of all, how do they help us learn its lessons?

 | DOI:10.1163/9789004385153_004

Testimonies of Injustice

When discussing the pain and suffering that occur under circumstances like those encountered during exile, we primarily refer to the experiences of a first person or a group of first persons, i.e., those who have suffered these abuses. All knowledge garnered from an experience and its suffering was, and is, unique. However, this uniqueness does not prevent each person from regularly attempting to connect with others by placing their experience with or against similar experiences that, among other catastrophes, continue to be repeated. The same first person, even while immersed in their particular suffering, does not stop searching for words to articulate it in relation to other experiences in the present or in the past, either of their own or of which they have knowledge. In other words, while suffering through life experiences, one also continues to "testify" to them. However, the first person does not recount their pain only to themself. They habitually confide in various second persons, allowing others to inform, as well as understand, the situation they are living or have lived. Of course, if given the opportunity after the fact, one looks to offer their account of these experiences. Humiliation compels (even more than honor). Testifying thus becomes a painful, inescapable matter of urgency. How should we approach knowledge that is based on testimony? What attitude should we adopt when confronted with these words?

We have seen that testimonial knowledge can typically be received through either a *principle of presumed trust* or a *principle of general credulity*. When finding testimonies that are as unique as testimonies of injustice, which of these two principles should we turn to?

The Difficult and Infuriating Art of Self-Interruption

For now, before discussing which principles should be followed when recovering information from exile experiences, we must make one thing clear. The moment people in exile (or any other situation involving forced actions) begin to recount their suffering, thus breaking the silence imposed by dictatorships and their internalized institutions of violence, it is time for us to suspend personal desires, beliefs and emotions and avoid the temptation to apply our own arrogant reasoning.

In such cases, we must learn to wait patiently for these confessions, or cries of grief, that are often expressed with great hesitance or rambling. It is not easy placing ourselves in situations that require abstaining from using our own words. We know that instead of letting the words of the victim speak for themselves, we naturally tend to "interpret" the victim or, as they say, "speak in their name," "represent" them. Or even worse, as has occurred in certain historical contexts, we enthusiastically seek to "totally take charge of the situation," and even "explain" the victim. The upsetting nature of these events provokes an arrogant application of reason, intervening to erect a barrier of words behind which we can conceal and, like absent-minded magicians, make the concrete suffering and injustice we are hearing disappear. Nevertheless, if we are to make the most of these embarrassing and disorienting moments, we must use them as exceptional incentives to practice an art that has been spurned because of the frustration it produces: *the art of self-interruption.*

What does such an art entail? For us to know how to listen, how to observe and even how to read, we must interrupt our customary reactions. Students of this art should (not without difficulty) practice living detached from themselves: they must provisionally, as much as possible, silence their interior voices, their expectations and disregard certain desires, beliefs, emotions and perhaps many of their own words. How can this art help us when dealing with testimonies of injustice, for example?

When victims offer their account of forced actions, and other actions taking place during displacements such as exile (as well as those of refugees or even worse, of death camp survivors), by recounting their pain and suffering, they are transmitting what Primo Levi aptly named the "raw material of indignation." What should we do with this "raw material"? Let me reiterate that we must practice the difficult and infuriating art of self-interruption and, before opening our mouths, we must allow ourselves to be overtaken by feelings of astonishment, incomprehension and pain.

Through these interruptions (actions we take against ourselves) that allow us to move closer to the one who is suffering or has suffered, both the victim's and our own subjectivities paradoxically recover their authority. (Not long ago was it not ceremoniously announced that the "subject," and even that "man" had died? Those were the days! *Sic transit gloria mundi* ...) With their return, intensely and even excessively subjective, first and second persons have once again moved to the forefront as sources of truth. Having survived a multitude of theoretical and often conflicting attacks—guided by diverse and contradictory notions of objectivity that managed to devour first and second persons—those first and second persons are not only again in possession of authentic experiences and able to act, but they are also capable of learning critical lessons.

But life goes on. As with any "raw material," this "raw material of indignation" will need to be dealt with one way or another. It is therefore unavoidable that we resume our discussion on knowledge. We must again ask ourselves what information a third person can trust when reconstructing exile's experiences and lessons, and which principles should be used to process this information.

Metatestimonies

For the moment, let us dispense with a common temptation. When we consider the knowledge that emerges *from* an exile experience, and we translate that into information *about* an experience—information that is both complex and entirely direct, and thus undeniably exact—we must immediately make a correction: no, the possibility of such information is not available to human animals. No, no such stable bedrock exists. The experiences of exile, like any other experience articulated using political cartography, are mediated by messy words arranged largely based on desires, emotions and interests. Even the most immediate bodily pain, like that inflicted by torture, is experienced one way or another according to the trauma of the desires, emotions and expectations of the individual suffering those horrible circumstances, whether they be religious, political or the result of a criminal's sudden rage. But why?

We have seen that a first person initiates a certain understanding or act of self-narration while living the experience, and all narration is realized using words which collaborate with perceptions. Simultaneous self-narration, as it constructs the person narrating, is itself constructed out of all other desires, beliefs and emotions emerging from that same narrator. At the same time, those narrative fragments advancing the first person's understanding, and self-understanding, mark the beginning of a process in which they must be understood again. Or, more accurately, one can always derive new interpretations from earlier narrations, for example, by introducing explanations for those events or approaching the events from an alternative perspective. Today, driven by fear one might commit certain actions that they think dishonor their exile, while tomorrow these same actions could be seen as displaying sound judgment and glimpses of an emerging wisdom which takes into account overlooked political implications. And so on, successively.

In this sense, knowledge from an exile testimony is made up of information selected by the first person (the one who offers their testimony) and the second person (the one who receives it), and both do so according to strategies shaped by their own desires, emotions and interests. Thus, when examining this information, we must not ignore our practical knowledge of these underlying selectors. To disregard their influence would likely result in considerable confusion, confusing the reasonable *principle of presumed trust* with the obscuring *principle of general credulity*.

Caveat: It would be a terrible misunderstanding to conclude from these observations on the constructed and therefore highly selective nature of all knowledge, including all testimonial knowledge, that testimonies of injustice do not merit our respect. Nothing could be further from their actual intention. I am only attempting to point out that the value of these testimonies does not increase, but instead decreases—sometimes drastically—when they are supported by allegedly simple and otherwise false presumptions about knowledge. Let us not forget: simplifying is often a trap, a loss of equilibrium.

We can now consider which testimonies among the countless ones available would best serve for learning about the experiences of exile. The first proposition presented stated that in ancient times the circumstances of exile were steeped in ambiguous prestige. On closer examination, one finds a moral knowledge in the Bible and schools of alternative Socratism (Aristippus, the Cynics, the Stoics ...) that seems to have been lost, or at least overshadowed, in modern times. This does not mean, however, that forced displacements have ceased. For us to recover those lessons, what "raw material of indignation" should we use: that which belongs to a past that is still present, but distant, or that which remains alive and well within current experiences? Do we really want to work with statistics, life stories, interviews, documentaries, fictional films or autobiographies written by a first person who chooses which stories they wish to tell?

Risking overindulgence, I present a *third proposition*: *if we intend to gather the remains of ancient knowledge of exile, as well as any specific knowledge provided by history, sociology, anthropology, political science and law, and then reinterpret it for the present day, that is, thoughtfully actualize it based on new experiences, then we should also experiment with the poetic word.*

In my defense, let us note that despite the fact that since Antiquity the world has continued to share (and sing) life stories of suffered forced displacements and has continued to write elegies, lamentations and hymns about these circumstances, there are, as far as I know, very few systematic moral, psychological and political investigations regarding exile.

For this reflection, allowing myself to get swept up in this third proposition and risking extreme partiality, I will use only atypical testimonies—i.e., verses—as evidence of exile experiences. These are testimonies that are metatestimonies: spontaneous confessions standing in contrast to memoirs, recorded life stories and even interviews and film documentaries that have been constructed by a certain deliberate individual subjectivity. Does such careful fabrication not distance these testimonies from that "raw material of indignation"?

By choosing to work with metatestimonies rather than testimonies, we will face words that have been displaced. Using practical knowledge and then explicitly employing various rhetorical techniques, metatestimonies are composed by taking both first-hand experiences as well as the testimonies of others as their "raw material." Such displacement presents a paradox that we would do well to keep in mind, a warning as we move forward: *the paradox of metatestimonies*. On the one hand, these are words bearing a signature: personalized language elaborated out of the desires, beliefs, emotions and expectations of a highly individual subjectivity. It would seem, then, that these are nothing more than personal confessions: intensely subjective constructions. On the other hand, these words produce artifacts that, as verses, aspire to free themselves from the "I" who spoke them; they seek to stand on their own. This is why when these metatestimonies are effective and accomplish their intended goal, the demands of subjectivity expressed therein as "nothing more than a personal confession" will give way to the introduction of a general perspective on certain "unsigned" life experiences. In this sense, even the most singular words applied to a singular exile can become vessels in which the experiences of a one's exile can be lived and recounted as belonging to a general type of experiences.

Testimonies and metatestimonies might consequently yield different outlooks depending on who is handling them. When an individual gives their testimony (a life story, a memoir, etc.), they are asking, "I want you to listen and to trust me. I give you my word." However, in the case of a metatestimony they are proposing, "Use this artifact that I am making available to you, these verses, for example, and examine whatever it is that you get from it."

Working with metatestimonies, rather than testimonies, especially in fields such as history, sociology, anthropology, political science and law, has the downside of inserting more distance between us and the lived experience, to use a pleonasm. The fact that these are artifacts made of carefully manipulated words could also cause considerable problems. These poems as artifacts do not come with an instruction manual explaining exactly how they work. Will we not get lost in dark corridors filled with the demands of a subjectivity that is too atypical, whether they be those of the one who created the artifacts or those of the one who activates them?

To answer this question, we must remember the metatestimonial paradox and some of its consequences. For example, with metatestimonies it is not wise to get overly mixed up in justifications, accusations or excuses like: "When I left I was filled with a terror you cannot know. I had the police at my heels. Therefore, what I have learned from exile is completely different." Such reactions can only lead us astray because unlike testimonies, metatestimonies have no intention of using transparency to communicate the details of a highly-personalized experience. Rather, they offer a performance of it, dramatizing it in an attempt to uncover a more-encompassing type of experience.

(Metatestimonies are not "dishonest." Sincerity is simply not a template that applies to them.)

For that same reason, metatestimonies of injustice allow for liberties—nuances, limits, discrepancies—not admitted and even disparaged by testimonies of injustice because of the personal suffering that these communicate. When we work with metatestimonies, we are less tempted to confuse the reasonable *principle of presumed trust* with the stifling *principle of general credulity* that prevents critical interrogation.

One more limitation in this investigation: from those hurried notes on several pieces of knowledge regarding exile in ancient times, I will jump ahead to the present. I do this heeding Nietzsche's warning that an investigation will contract the antiquarian's illnesses if, at some point, it does not address personal concerns and somehow embrace the personal interests of the investigator. Or what is worse, anyone who becomes too concerned with distant suffering and ignores the catastrophes close to home would inevitably be accused of hypocrisy.

I accept a certain desire to remain close to my own circumstances and, despite working with metatestimonies, I am conscious not to distance myself too much from that "raw material of indignation." Therefore, the few metatestimonies that I will examine belong to an immediately *present past*, a memory that is still living: the Spanish Republic's massive exile during and following the Spanish Civil War in the first half of the twentieth century and the exiles of Latin America's Southern Cone (Argentina, Chile and Uruguay), products of sinister dictatorships that devastated the region in the second half of the twentieth century.

There is no question that both exiles were different and reflect historically different causes. Nevertheless, by relating the demands of subjectivity expressed by these metatestimonies, besides risking transatlantic studies (to use a pretentious term), I am able to highlight connections between them that are difficult to deny: in many cases we are dealing with cultural structures and institutions that for various Latin American countries are united through multiple generations of the same family, in universities, in schools, in political groups, in publishing houses and in journals. Also, since we are working with poems, it is important to note the diverse articulations of a shared Spanish language used in these metatestimonies.

The desire for proximity should not, however, cause us to get sidetracked down dead-end paths. Reflection can also connect these considerations of relatively recent memories with the ancient remains of the knowledge summoned by the exiles of Antiquity. There is, in fact, much to be gained from this. Let us look again at the experiences and lessons expressed in various books of the Bible, in the Greek schools of thought that I have placed together under the name "alternative Socratism," in the poetry of Ovid and in the meditations of Roman Stoicism.

From such varied materials, even at a glance we can distinguish certain recurring categories related to the notion of self. For example, in the Book of Lamentations, in various Psalms or in Ovid, exile is experienced as devastating loss: a growing melancholy from having been forced to abandon something of great, perhaps the greatest, importance. In contrast, in the Books of Jeremiah and Ezekiel exile is a school for learning how to resist evil and wrongdoing. We encounter other, perhaps contrary but no less evident, forms of resistance when Aristippus, the Cynics and some Stoics reject even their most treasured relationships. On the other hand, the conclusions of Jeremiah's and Ezekiel's prophecies and the songs of Deutero-Isaiah, in particular, are invaded by imminent redemption: we are invited to let ourselves be carried away—even if just for a moment—by winds heralding unforeseen horizons. Such convictions, those which place us at the threshold of a new way of life, are also frequent, albeit in a different sense, in Aristippus, the Cynics and in the calm and reasoned approach of Stoic cosmopolitanism: their "at any moment, in any place, if I wish, I can open a door, any door and be at home."

With these cursory observations in mind, I now present a *fourth proposition* that will lead us to exile's direct lessons without any further delay: *if we examine the most diverse stories, we will undoubtedly be surprised by how overwhelming the evidence is that certain types of experiences, for example, exile as loss, exile as resistance and exile as a new beginning, are found in the most diverse locations and the most diverse time periods.*

An initial investigation into possible lessons in exile is not the place to carry out the scholarly historical, sociological, anthropological, political-scientific and legal inquiries necessary to properly substantiate this fourth proposition. For the time being, I only wish to point out that each of these types of experiences—loss, resistance, new beginnings—continues to be found in many poems from the Spanish Republican exile as well as those from the Latin American Southern Cone exiles of the sixties and seventies. (Also, let us not forget that it will be important for us to use these materials toward the end of this reflection in the reconstruction of a perspective, exile as a perspective, that will also allow us access to exile's indirect lessons on culture, morality and people.)

Following this (perhaps irresponsible) method of reading various verses as metatestimonies, I will then begin, after so many detours, to recover several of exile's direct lessons. After all, the third proposition that I presented appears to consider it not so unreasonable to venture the following challenge (or promise): "Tell me what verses you sing, listen to, write or read, and I will tell you who you are."

Or maybe this proposition assumes a much greater challenge because it implicates us in unanticipated ramifications: “Entrust me with some of the verses that you and those around you sing, listen to, write and read, and I will not only know your experiences and the lessons you learned, but presumably several decisive fragments of human life as well, including how one lives it and how one wants to live it.”

CHAPTER 3

Exile as Loss

Experiencing your misfortune as a form of abandonment. Suffering a vague but persistent feeling of helplessness. Believing that there is no place for you in society. These are the frequent companions of exile that lurk in the shadows. From this one might conclude, not without a hint of irritation and perhaps even disgust: "Exiles represent a class of socially incapacitated individuals."

Incapacitated: what could be more natural than for those who have been forced to leave behind the shelter of familiar landscapes for strange new horizons (including language or the accent of a language that is unrecognizable to their childhood memories) to feel disoriented and, immediately or over time, obsessively worthless and lacking in abilities?

What options does one have besides seeking refuge inside the suffering inflicted by these forced actions? It has been sung countless times and in many languages: in exile, what else can one do but lock oneself inside the pieces of one's own broken heart? This is why the grief stemming from loss is almost without exception the first type of experience that visits, tempts and seduces the exile. It should come as no surprise that this attitude is one of the most persistent authors of poems on exile, especially of those that are also composed in exile.

What follows now is a portrait of exile experienced only as loss. It is characterized by melancholic—painfully melancholic—behavior whose essential conviction is: "Everything that matters is in ruins." This is the first property of exile as loss. The second property of this exile experience is that the individual will staunchly embrace their melancholy. Driven by desperation, they seek to make their suffering a permanent way of life.

Such reactions are not without good reason, as we will come to see. When the things one loves the most are taken away and one is flung into adversity, or simply into the unknown, it is not uncommon to feel rejected, even devastated. In the case of exile, each day the outside world forges a path made with complex constellations of absences: people, livelihoods, ideals, causes, traditions, stories. In turn, each one of these absences alludes to moments of joy, sadness, generosity, jealousy, grief, indignation and ways that they were able to react to situations when familiarity offered shelter and security. Back then one knew where and how to walk, but not anymore. Now each step makes it clear to the exile that this is precisely what they are: a foreigner, often stuttering incomprehensible words in hopes of getting a job that they had never wanted.

 | DOI:10.1163/9789004385153_005

Forced into a state of foreignness, from then on they will have to learn to live alongside a smokescreen, that existent or approaching statement, "Be grateful for what we offer you! If you feel that what we give you is not enough, if it is not to your liking, then go back to where you came from!" Indeed, a first person's first steps into exile typically bring them face to face with dark uncertain corners that, as such, may and frequently do contain exterior and secret interior enemies capable of pushing them over the edge.

That is why refusing to allow oneself to grieve and to complain, eluding or repressing the first property of those who experience exile as loss (that painful melancholy), leads to a denial of what has truly taken place. What is more, an individual incapable of mourning amidst catastrophe is condemned to never know where they are or how they got there. Among many other consequences, they refuse to allow themselves to learn from the unpredictable teacher we call "history," cruel in its lack of compassion.

Nevertheless, from the perspective of involuntary goodbyes that exile imposes, not only does one suffer for what has happened, and maybe continues to happen, but this suffering also often comes to be revered, and one assigns a certain value to its permanence. Suffering can even be framed as a sign of great character—the second property of exile experienced as loss. Thus, suffering tends to become a badge of honor pinned upon a bleeding chest and worn for the rest of one's life. Relying on this sorrow, the voice in Psalm 137 commands:

> If I forget thee, O Jerusalem, let my right hand forget its skill
> Let my tongue cling to the roof of my mouth if I do not remember thee
> if I do not exalt Jerusalem above my chief joy.

Ovid also declares this unending pain to be the only attitude capable of honoring everything that has been lost. The words used in the tradition of exile experienced only as loss are commonly dictated by infinite spirals of desperation that know no solace. Or rather, they believe to know for a fact that there is no solace. If I am not mistaken, many of these experiences can be analyzed as the result of successive conflicts between interior and exterior worlds. They are conflicts between subjectivity and the new realities that inescapably continue to surround it.

One way of provoking these conflicts arises by equating everything of importance in the exterior world with the lost homeland, which in turn begins to fade away into the interior world. In 1939, for example, Pedro Garfias jotted down the twenty-two poems of his *Spring in Eaton Hastings* [*Primavera en Eaton Hastings*] while in England after the defeat of the Spanish Republic. The first person in these poems grabs hold of his misery with all his might through constantly fluctuating emotions that transform an eclogue into an elegy and an elegy into a longing for emptiness, a longing for nothing. The subtitle of the work suggests just such a descent: *Bucolic Poem with Intervals of Weeping* [*Poema bucólico con intermedios de llanto*]. A terrifying realization: the quiet English park in Eaton Hastings where the exile is sitting is completely removed from the Spanish catastrophe, which results in his progressive isolation. As he barricades himself inside this intimacy, a circumstance that has been imposed on him—but also to some degree chosen—the exterior world dissipates and is substituted, almost to the tiniest detail, by an inner world full of loved and hated phantasmagorias that are largely a product of that very act of isolation. For this reason, any solace experienced in the exterior world seems unreal and gradually disappears, giving way to rage as one eventually decides: "You are no longer important, you no longer matter."

> I can populate you, my solitude,
> just as I can make rocks and trees
> from these dark people who encircle me.[1]

If this description of the privations of exile is fulfilled, one descends, so to speak, into the labyrinth of natural history: the first person transforms the others, those people surrounding him, into vegetables and minerals. This descent where one finds oneself completely alone among rocks and trees may be the only means of enduring what is so terrifying: the continued proliferation of absence. Note that the voice in this exile metatestimony has nothing in particular against those people. It is not because they are English that they are called "dark people." They are "dark people" because they are not "his" people. They are not the Spaniards that he left behind in those faraway places he considered to be his own. In exile poems like this one, there are two alternating worlds in conflict: the idyllic present, life safe and sound in a location protected by what we tend to call the "remains of civilization" but which no longer exists for this type of exile or else is slowly evaporating, versus their raging memory filled with atrocities and remnants of the brutality they suffered, which is what matters most to them.

This agony can even destroy the conflict between exterior and interior worlds by silencing all other voices except one: that of one's own past. More and more, the person's new surroundings represent a space located beyond any worthwhile effort. No second person is capable of reaching them now that

1 "Yo te puedo poblar, soledad mía, / igual que puedo hacer rocas y árboles / de estas oscuras gentes que me cercan."

they have progressively become exiled inside themselves. It is not surprising, then, that an elaborate rite of non-hospitality is carried out, redefining the limits of the world to correspond to the limits of one's own solitude. Regardless of what happens,

> and still I would continue to see in its unscathed whiteness,
> who knows, maybe sleeping, the Spain I have lost.[2]

Out of the growing darkness and that rising wall of shadows comes the "unscathed whiteness" of absence, an allusion to the vast treasures left behind. Perhaps such bright words as these can be used because the exile has placed themself somewhere other than within the travails of daily life, other than the ebb and flow between despair and hopeful effort, between small accomplishments and small defeats.

From Mexico, a land possibly less foreign since it is inhabited by articulations of the same language, José Moreno Villa takes another step in the process of interiorizing values held to be decisive. In the poem "Your Land" ["Tu tierra"] he devastatingly notes:

> Your land lies beyond the water.
> Never will your eyes see it again.[3]

As on so many occasions, words again give in when facing impossible desires. Or rather, one raises walls which, although imagined, are no less impossible to scale. "Beyond the water" is a way of saying "beyond anything that matters," and even "beyond any possible life." These words are not addressing those people around the first person. To whom, then, are they speaking? At whom are they shouting? At the past, each moment more filled with illusions.

Certainly, for the voice pronouncing these words, accepting some of the new people that exile has put them in contact with would imply betraying the person that they were before, the person that they have been until that moment. But are days and nights not founded on just such "betrayals," establishing new relationships with the people who by chance and often by surprise cross our path? From time to time doubts arise as to whether or not it makes sense to identify oneself so steadfastly with what was, with the stolen homeland:

---

2 "y aún seguiría viendo con su blancura intacta, / quién sabe si dormida, la España que he perdido."

3 "Yace tu tierra más allá del agua. / Nunca tus ojos volverán a verla."

> That land of yours—they will tell you—is made of dust,
> like every other homeland in the world.[4]

But these doubts are quickly pushed aside, as if refusing to equate the world with the homeland were an unforgivable act of sacrilege. Yet, would not such a refusal only lead to fear? Maybe this is why such doubts are rejected, attaching to it an unrelenting "never":

> But no. Your land is the absolute
> formula of your being.[5]

An observer unfamiliar with these regrets might declare, not without a certain air of sarcasm (irony that shows no pity or sympathy): "Since there is no difference between you and your land, then you are not really here, in your new circumstances, in the same place as your body and the possibility of new experiences that might force you to modify your desires, your beliefs, your emotions. Everything you owned was left buried there beyond the water, in the "unscathed whiteness" of your nostalgia. You are almost a corpse now. This is no longer about you having lost all of your possessions. You have lost yourself. Your entire being inhabits a dimension of loss."

One may take this one step further and proclaim that it is not just the exterior world that has been destroyed in exile, but the interior world as well. Thus, neither the exterior nor interior worlds matter because nothing of value remains; there is nothing that could, or should, inspire any interest. The Latin American exile in the sixties and seventies has most certainly known this despair. For example, following the defeat of the Chile's Popular Unity political alliance, Gonzalo Millán notifies us in his poem "The City" ["La ciudad"] that a large part of the population has been decapitated. Borrowing Pablo Neruda's well-known image of the "tree of the people," he transforms the exiled person into debris, a broken branch:

> They cut off our heads.
> They cut down the tree.
> They dismembered us.
> They chopped up the trunk.
> They cut off the branches.[6]

---

4 "Ésa tu tierra—te dirán—es de polvo, / como todas las patrias del mundo."

5 "Pero, no. Tu tierra es la fórmula / archicompleta de tu ser."

6 "Nos descabezaron. / Talaron el árbol. / Nos descuartizaron. / Trozaron el tronco. / Cortaron las ramas."

Let us pause to reflect for a moment. By experimenting with these few verses, accepting their challenges and responding to them in different ways, we have witnessed a flight towards de-personalization when exile is experienced only as loss. One cause setting this (frightening) process in motion is the disappearance, whether real or imaginary, of the second person, both in their singular and plural forms. Of course, in the end the first person also disappears; without any support from a fellow human being, the first person eliminates itself. I will again retrace that stifling practice of bidding farewell to oneself which begins with somber confessions like:

– I am still somebody because someone else believes so, even if that someone is absent.

Soon comes another step in that farewell:

– I am still somebody even if nobody else believes so.

But sooner or later, and almost unavoidably, in a swift sleight of self-destruction one stumbles across a bitter realization:

– I am nobody.

Is there nothing left, then? Perhaps the answer to this question is that only the illusion that nothing is left still remains. All traces of reality have been dissolved with the loss. There is only nobody, nothing: branches cut off and soon to be carried away by the next storm. The fact that the exile is often condemned to live among absences, which we have already seen in many compelling passages from the Bible, makes each poem into an artifact wanting only to produce a series of irrefutable words, words that end up articulating just that: testaments.

Testament: one's last, definitive will. A declaration drawn up from the final will of an individual and which establishes what must be done with their belongings. In this case, it can perhaps be taken as a declaration of how certain losses should be understood or perhaps even how memory and life should be understood.

This tradition of the testament seemingly becomes almost mandatory when, in the heat of the early stages (their initial experiences) of exile, the first person decides to speak. This tradition, which relies on the two properties of exile experienced as loss (painful melancholy and its indefinite permanence), establishes the image of the exiled individual within the tradition itself as well as in the eyes of those who receive them time and again: those who meet them with hospitality, indifference, hatred or with various combinations of all three.

Looking to react against these testaments, the plural title of Ida Vitale's poem "Exiles" ["Exilios"], implying that all exiles having something in common, attempts to neutralize experiences that cling too tightly to what has been lost, as if to mitigate any ambitious prestige sought for the experience of exile. What is more, this metatestimony, written in Mexico in the seventies after fleeing the dictatorship in her country of Uruguay, takes on a third-person point of view. Such a choice suggests an effort to not fall into the trap of any *principle of general credulity* and to observe meticulously, perhaps unsympathetically, those (maybe herself included) who live exile as loss. It reminds us that sometimes allowing oneself to sink in the misfortunes of exile leads to the destruction of a possible history yet to be lived. The first fragments of the poem describe these poor souls:

> They are here and there: on their way,
> nowhere.
> Each horizon: where an ember entices.
> They could walk towards any crevice.
> There is no compass, no voices.
>
> They cross deserts that the fierce sun
> or the frost burn
> and infinite fields without the limit
> that makes them real,
> that would almost make them of earth and grass.[7]

The exile is situated between two places, in a "between" that is a "non-place." But for one who experiences exile as categorical loss, this is not a momentary "non-place" (not a hotel stay, not a voyage, not a curable disease). Instead, it is a "non-place" of residence produced at the intersection of two opposing tendencies, or rather, in their realization: the unrelenting tension between the exceptional nature that one uncomfortably acquires and the almost uninterrupted invisibility that one lives. What is involved in this notion of self?

Exceptionality is, by definition, what stands apart from the ordinary, what breaks the rule. Exceptionality invades, unsettles and even destroys normality. This is why exceptionality must acquire such a vast presence; I would almost venture to say that it can only survive in a climate of its emphatic self-presentation. Vitale's poem condemns the exile's supposed exceptionality as illusory. We do not usually encounter exceptionality in exile—only desires, beliefs and extreme emotions: exaggerations that are mistaken as exceptional.

7 "Están aquí y allá: de paso, / en ningún lado. / Cada horizonte: donde un ascua atrae. / Podrían ir hacia cualquier grieta. / No hay brújula ni voces. // Cruzan desiertos que el bravo sol / o que la helada queman / y campos infinitos sin el límite / que los vuelve reales, / que los haría casi de tierra y pasto."

In exile, everything is *too much*: the sun is "fierce," the frost "burns," the fields are "infinite." As if it were necessary, this realm of excess (the "unscathed whiteness" in Garfias' poem, Moreno Villa's no less definitive "never will your eyes see it again," or Millán's apocalyptic tone) confirms that we have cut all ties with the practices of history: those endless and at times insignificant, exhausting, constraining or boring tasks that can also hide small nourishing, comforting surprises. Because, indeed, beyond this panic-filled language, each morning involves us confronting and, frequently, surpassing the limits of certain reasonably-defined fields: "the limit / that makes them real, / that would almost make them of earth and grass."

By adopting the third-person point of view, the pain of exile is reinterpreted in this metatestimony as an abundance of exaggerated gestures spiraling centripetally. Those movements, all of them ultimately meaningless, dissolve into an aimless succession of steps, into ruinous sorrow (that rueful mixture of self-compassion and maliciousness disguised as exhaustion): "They could walk towards any crevice. / There is no compass, no voices."

A consequence of this tension between purported exceptionality and actual invisibility can be articulated as the *paradox of persevering excitement*: approaching an experience with an exaggerated degree of excitement conceals an increasingly deteriorated emotional state.

Furthermore, in this tradition of exile metatestimonies where loss is experienced as absolute, each and every second person of any significance, enemy or friend, is absent; sadly, even those of no importance to us are absent. Thus, the exile's weary, defenseless gaze builds bridges to nowhere, toward no one. They do not seek help, much less attention or affection. They have been damaged to the extent that they do not allow themselves to feel rage or hatred, not even toward their enemies. These are gazes that find no mutual understanding in the gazes of others. These are gazes that have forbidden themselves from the start from ever being reached by a "you" or from reaching out to a "you." Since there is no friendly "you," or unfriendly "you," or indifferent "you," because there is no more "you," only the muted echoes of an exterior world in a steady state of depopulation remain; only a thickening fog producing progressively hopeless movements on the way to eventual paralysis.

By refusing to engage in acts of new social identifications and counteridentifications, one who experiences exile only as loss ceases to live as a part of history: that frustrating march onward which for worse, and sometimes for better, deviates from our desired course. The exile becomes socially incapacitated, wandering about the prison of their memory. Anyone incapable of facing a second person's acceptance or exclusion of them, brings about their own annihilation, whether it be by placing others "beyond the waters" to eliminate in advance any possibility of new acquaintances or non-acquaintances or by transforming others into vegetables or minerals that do nothing more than "encircle" the first person.

At this point in the reflection we must begin to ask what possible lessons the experiences we have collected here can teach us? The testaments of Garfias, Moreno Villa and Millán are expressed in verses written in the first person. On the other hand, Vitale's artifact, constructed with deliberate distance, uses the point of view of a cautious third person to skillfully reveal the dangers of that conduct. If the first person insists on identifying itself entirely with their homeland, if they see it as the "absolute formula of your being" and remove the possibility of learning—that generator of new days—to a location "beyond the waters," then they are exacting their own ruin, permanently.

A (possibly improper) question might arise if we were to consider a (possibly irrelevant) detail in this metatestimony: that the person who produced this lucid artifact, with their displaced gaze, is a woman. "A woman!" perhaps exclaimed with naive admiration. It is well known that women have been socially constructed throughout history to be little more than props for complicated and capricious love affairs. Why then is this human animal who is hardly capable of abstraction and, on top of that, in exile, exclusively assuming a third person point of view? She rakes our eyes with these pointed truths: if we allow ourselves to be carried away by certain demands of our subjectivity and, as a result, take up residence inside our loss, then we are inviting misery upon ourselves and surrendering to it entirely.

With this we reach a first type of exile's direct lessons.

There Is a Time to Be Involved and a Time to Step Away

This is a precarious lesson because it requires two mindsets that not only point in opposing directions, but also frequently enter into bitter conflicts that are often difficult to resolve.

On the one hand, anyone who does not intensely, even excessively, assume the first property of exile experienced as loss—i.e., anyone in exile who has not discovered that painful melancholy—will become nothing more than an inattentive tourist who, fed up with so much struggle, has decided to be only a photographer of the surrounding events without allowing themself to be affected by them. Anyone in exile, or in any other catastrophe, who does not feel concerned is either not fully aware or completely ignorant of what has happened to them and, thus, is not fully aware or is completely ignorant of who they are.

On the other hand, sooner or later one must also be capable of suppressing the second property of exile experienced as loss and avoid transforming the mourning period into a permanent state. We must not objectify a bottomless plunge into melancholy, for anyone who is incapable of taking a step backward and adopting a third person point of view in order to better understand their place of suffering will forever remain a prisoner in their orgies of hyperbole. They will fall victim to their own arrogant reasoning, which will lead them to confuse exceptionality with excess, and bravery with affectation. Such confusion is but one of the many conundrums in which our fantasy can indulge.

However, are there certain norms that might assist us in measuring to what extent we should be involved in our loss and at what point it would be best to step away? To better frame this first type of lesson in exile, I will revert to several vague generalities that we have already mentioned: without courageously assuming the first-person point of view, there can be no genuine experience of history (where else can we live but in the historical first person, unless it is in fantasy?). Besides, during an action and, at some point, during an experience, I am bound to come face to face with a second person, singular or plural, imaginary or, many times, real. And despite the protection of my many well-placed traps, a third person point of view will also appear, inevitably calling into question the *principle of general credulity*. But how can one learn to dismiss those crippling worries, those visions overly concerned with themselves. The actions and experiences of anyone refusing to quiet their first-person point of view—to practice the art of self-interruption—impeding any intervention from a second person, will drown inside their own malleability; they will become arbitrary and, eventually, incomprehensible. The individual will no longer be able to distinguish belief from whim, desire from action, emotion from deception. When certain actions and experiences are left to their own design, they tend toward a single shared direction, steeped in terrible melodrama as they vertiginously dig themselves into a bottomless pit.

Let us, then, be cautious with individual and collective memories of suffering. While they may offer us support in the beginning, there comes a point when they will begin to consume us, as described by the *paradox of persevering excitement*. It is no coincidence that in most cases when recounting exile only as loss, we attempt to create the illusion that time has stopped and that history no longer exists. Or we believe, or attempt to believe, that it has been eliminated. Or, to be more precise, we act as if such a thing had occurred even if we do not entirely believe it. Only through such a maneuver as this is it possible for us to proclaim that we have lost everything, that there is no future. Just as with other temporary or feigned deaths, these also hide certain illusory forms of power that mask raging impotence. For this reason, when an experience is described as absolute loss, it is in fact an indication that the experience is in need of a new description. To live is to allow ourselves to change.

We must be open to notions of ourselves that include complex and risky practices. It is important to learn to be inside history, weeping and yelling until we are hoarse, even wandering the earth with our heart in pieces: the first reaction of those experiencing exile as loss.

Yet, at some point (when?), however great the momentum may be, however difficult it may be to bring this downward spiral to a halt, one must know how to resist the prestige of the abyss by appealing to the art of self-interruption. This step backward allows us to notice the roar of the outside world; in particular, the complaints, insults, wishes, demands, greetings, judgments, moans and blessings of those who are out there with us: the second reaction, both contrary and complementary to the first, of those hoping to learn from exile experienced as loss. We must not barricade the doors and windows in order to become victims of ourselves and make sorrow our final resting place. Let us not forget that the expression "final resting place" prompts various unrelenting attacks on life itself.

CHAPTER 4

Exile as Resistance

Counter to the tradition of suffering exile as loss, where mourning and melancholy are unremitting, is that of exile confronted as resistance, sounding its brave rallying cry. But why does this tradition involve a rallying cry? And why is it brave? Like exile as loss, living exile as resistance consists of two properties: first, behavior that is partly reactive and partly active, and second, behavior that suggests and fosters courage.

Resisting forced actions usually leads to a clear exclamation of dissent, a *no*. Consequently, we attempt to react against an established order or disorder. However, what is most at stake is our own identity, our concern for the protection of a certain notion we have of ourselves. Through resistance we manage to continue being different from what the powers we are resisting wish us to be.

Furthermore, resisting implies both courage and anger: courage in the determination to see an undertaking through to its end, and anger in the intensity of the emotions involved. (For example, "I cannot help but feel angry about how I am being treated" or "I cannot help but feel angry knowing that they continue to impose their will on me!")

Words like "resist" and "resistance" are usually accompanied by an epic dialect of allusions whose roar serves to overcome memories of terror and suffering, and to recognize one's ability to march faithfully into battle, enthusiastically and without fear. We shall limit the uses of these prestigious words to moral and political contexts, which are the most relevant when stating that one lives, or that one should live, exile as resistance. Keep in mind that the word "resist" denotes not allowing oneself to be moved or influenced by a power considered to be negative ("to fight against a dictatorship," "to not yield to the temptation of getting too comfortable"). At the same time, "not allowing oneself" implies not giving in to whoever attacks us ("they fought the tyrant on all fronts"). In particular, the condition of resistance suggests the ability to endure without succumbing ("I don't know how they could endure such torture and not talk"). In each case, the distinctive features of resisting seem to produce precise, decisive behaviors: one "reacts forcefully against" some power whose goal is to make us different from what we want to be.

There are many different ways of not submitting to those powers attempting to reshape a first person against their will, depending upon the social situation and the demands of one's subjectivity. At one extreme lies the decision to fight

 | DOI:10.1163/9789004385153_006

without the slightest prospect of surrender or to refuse to cooperate in any way with what has been identified as the evil that must be fought. At the other extreme are those minute daily dissents—silent, but stubborn and effective.

Often, we find well-reasoned expressions of resistance within the tradition of exile as loss. This resistance even tends to appear as a product of the tradition of loss. However, we only discover them once words are no longer laden with nostalgia or traces of bitterness and instead are being used to establish a social horizon with that temperament so characteristic of human animals: persevering in our dissent, enduring the hurricanes raging against us without a hint of cowardice.

In Rafael Alberti's *Ballads and Songs of the Paraná* [*Baladas y canciones del Paraná*] (published for the first time in Buenos Aires in 1954, almost 15 years after the start of his exile in Argentina), there is no lack of suffering for the many things that have been left behind. An unmistakable longing for the lands and people of Spain permeates this poetry. Yet, out of every verse arises a need to transform that longing into an act of resistance.

Throughout Song 17 we hear a harsh pronouncement against anyone who experiences exile only as loss. The first words are governed by a firmly negative "not … not." These verses rebel against the reduction of sadness to states of mourning that transform us into statues of salt. They insist that any melancholy should not eliminate the possibility of future encounters with the unexpected:

> Sadness is not despair.
> It is not the negation of life.[1]

Soon afterwards, the main stanza explains the reasoning behind this rectification. With our sadness, we can also forge an instrument for rising up against those who have brought this punishment and subjection upon us. We learn that suffering, when reclaimed correctly, can offer remedies for the victim's recovery:

> Because of the profound sadness
> for what man has experienced,
> man can break mountains,[2]

Anyone determined to resist will eventually discover cracks within the losses through which it is possible to press forward. And when that "raw material of indignation" takes charge of our sadness, it does not lead to a bitterness seeking refuge inside itself, like the snail left to be trampled. Instead, it becomes its

1 "La tristeza no es desánimo. / No es negación de la vida."
2 "Por la profunda tristeza / de lo que el hombre ha pasado, / puede el hombre romper montes,"

opposite: reasons that serve as spears for battle. Unexpectedly, perhaps, Alberti's ballad proposes how one can generate resistance out of sadness, a material so poorly suited to such a task:

> My sadness is anger, it is wrath,
> rage, fury, passion.[3]

All but hidden at the end of this work by Alberti, almost as an appendix, we find "Ballad of the Man Who Never Went to Granada" ["Balada del que nunca fue a Granada"], which, when sung to the accompaniment of Paco Ibáñez' guitar, became one of the hymns in many events organized by Spanish exiles. The density of these verses lies in the fact that they depict the overlapping remains of memories both from the near present and a distant past. On the one hand, the words seem to evoke the fifteenth-century forced exodus of the Jews and Moors from Granada and an old man who remembers it. In his longing for a world from which he will possibly forever be excluded (which varies throughout successive pairs of verses), a third verse ceremoniously exclaims: "I never went to / saw / entered ... Granada."[4] One might argue that the expulsion of the Jews and Moors from what is now known as Spain alludes to ancient history—only a faint shadow, if indeed any shadow remains. Not at all. We know that this shadow has returned to wander through our streets and through our lives once again. And this time not even as vaporous ghosts, but rather as disgraced people of flesh and bone demanding, sometimes violently ... What is it that they are demanding?

When this poem was written, there were other relatively recent events flowing through the painful stories of Jewish and Muslim exiles—the assassination of Federico García Lorca: "Blood has spilled from our greatest brother."[5] Even so, despite the fact that the entire poem was built upon a verse by Lorca, the feeling of desolation does not end in destruction. On the contrary, it is an invitation to revolt. The final words challenge this suffering through an act of affirmative resistance and something more. Courage regains its composure to formulate a promise:

> Though the towers are high, so is our valor.
> Come through mountains, by seas and over fields.
> I will enter Granada.[6]

---

3 "Mi tristeza es ira, es rabia, / cólera, furia, arrebato."

4 "Nunca fui a / vi / entré en... Granada."

5 "Hay sangre caída del mejor hermano."

6 "Si altas son las torres, el valor es alto. / Venid por montañas, por mares y campos. / Entraré en Granada."

Similar to Alberti's poems, we recognize an attitude that is at the same time reactive and active in verses from the Southern Cone, which in the seventies began to articulate exile as resistance. Notably, the Uruguayan Mario Benedetti made resistance a matter of honor in poems that are like pamphlets for his militancy. More than metatestimonies, Benedetti's verses present us with manifestos to be sung in chorus, rather than hummed silently in solitude.

Benedetti's systems of belonging are clearly defined. As a witness to the Río de la Plata dictatorships, he often informs us of the social and political circumstances that he was forced to endure. His songs cry out while also urging us to participate in the protest. Unsurprisingly, he utilizes simple and direct language written in enjambed verses to greater accentuate the colloquial tone. In the following proclamation from *Everyday Poems* (1978–1979) [*Cotidianas* (1978–1979)], which Benedetti wrote in exile, we are quickly encouraged to equate "resist" with "exist":

> I'm going with the skittish
> lizard
> to visit the prison cells where...[7]

From there, names are hurled out into the emptiness as if attempting to decorate it with small black and white photos that might awaken the blurred memories of individuals who resisted. And since the reader is likely unaware of the context in which they were taken, these worn images can be nothing more that: depictions of people who resisted. Nevertheless, this endless naming of unfamiliar prisoners is not just trying to counter the passing of time by recording their footprints in words. By filling the air with these names, it is showing respect and gratitude to those resisting or who succeeded in resisting:

> I'm going with the people's
>
> lizard
> skittish
> to leave for them here and there
> through the bars
> beside their scars
> or in their spoons
> crumbs of respect

7 "Me voy con la lagartija / vertiginosa / a recorrer las celdas donde ...."

trust-filled silences

and gratitude for their existence.[8]

The poetry of the Argentinian Juan Gelman, like that of Alberti and Benedetti, is born out of the tradition of exile as loss, where exiled life feels like a branch that has been sawed off or a flame that has been extinguished. However, also like in Alberti and Benedetti, Gelman's words venture into the tradition of resistance. The following poem—which at one point was one of the most popular in Argentina during the second half of the twentieth century, a sort of *ars poetica* for living exile as resistance—presents a deceptively simple proclamation:

My Beloved Buenos Aires

Seated at the edge of a broken-through chair,
dizzy, sick, almost alive,
I write verses previously wept
for the city where I was born.

Catch them, catch them, also here
sweet children of mine were born
who sweeten life beautifully during such punishment.
One must learn to resist.

Not to leave or to stay,
to resist,
though it is certain
that still more suffering and forgetting lie ahead.[9]

The title and tone hint at mournful melodrama replete with resentment and weeping, and with no end in sight according the final verse. But unlike Benedetti's pamphlets, Gelman's words do more than just invite us to sing along.

8 "voy con la lagartija // popular / vertiginosa / a dejarles aquí y allá / por entre los barrotes / junto a las cicatrices / o sobre la cuchara / migas de respeto / silencios de confianza // y gracias porque existen."

9 "*Mi Buenos Aires querido*: Sentado al borde de una silla desfondada, mareado, enfermo, casi vivo, / escribo versos previamente llorados / por la ciudad donde nací. // Atrápalos, atrápalos, también aquí / nacieron hijos dulces míos / que entre tanto castigo te endulzan bellamente. / Hay que aprender a resistir. // Ni a irse ni a quedarse, / a resistir, / aunque es seguro / que habrá más penas y olvido."

They also dismantle a well-known tango made popular by Carlos Gardel. It needs no musical accompaniment; the music is already buried inside the verses. As I mentioned, however, this is a deceptively simple proclamation. The various parts of the poem remain disconnected, not easily fitting together. What does this mean?

A voice in the first person drags itself through the first stanza. Anyone hearing it would think it had reached the end of its existence, inconsolably "at the edge." The shade of its words could not be any darker: the misery and abandonment of a "broken-through chair," the liminal state of one who feels "dizzy, sick," and then the hyperbolic "almost alive." What is more, these words were not previously thought up, but rather, they were "wept." Why? To what end?

Perhaps it is because the dignity referred to in the well-worn expression "original state of one who confesses in this way" has transformed into despair: the "city where I was born" has become uninhabitable. To what then can this first person remain loyal? The opening four verses in the first person describe a way of life bordering on the most irrational manifestation of the first tradition of exile: misery reveling in its own incessant suffering.

However, this artifact that Gelman has created is also an exercise in the art of self-interruption: in a sudden fit of insolence it makes an about-face, landing a cunning blow to jolt the reader to attention. In the first three verses of the second stanza, a second person steps forward to rebuke the first person with an ambiguous anaphora: "Catch them …" Catch who? We are told that there has been weeping and punishment, but also sweetness, like a flame still flickering although buried. Where? In the days and nights of that painful past? And then yet another surprise: in the final five verses a different voice is heard, one that assumes the third person in order to somberly communicate a moral and political duty: "One must learn to resist." We might argue, "is this not a typical immediate reaction?" Not at all. The experience through which we learn to stand up against injustice and to not remain indifferent is filled with obstacles. It is a difficult task to continue one's dissent once the consequences of this action have become clear. For this reason, one must exercise courage: the second property of resistance.

What alternative is there for the person who refuses the moral and political lesson of saying no, of resisting? According to these verses, it will be one of two outcomes that typically follow a seizure of power. That is, either one must passively accept defeat by staying or one must bear defeat actively by leaving. Thus, this metatestimony proclaims that resistance is the only way to not accept defeat, whether by staying or leaving. These words can be read as a distant echo of the Golden Age Spanish poet Lope de Vega regarding the dilemmas that lay waste to our days in the continuous strain of irreconcilable desires:

Departing but to stay, and staying to depart;
To leave soulless, bearing the soul of another.[10]

On the other hand, we must be cautious of political resistance because it offers us very few guarantees if we do not allow ourselves to be deceived by fantastic stories proposing outrageous utopias. Unlike Gardel's tango "My Beloved Buenos Aires" and its happy ending where "there will be no more suffering or forgetting," any clearheaded political resistance understands that the negations in this verse can easily disappear due to that inelegant thing we call "social circumstances." Without a doubt, history has much more suffering and much more forgetting in store for us.

Anyone not allowing themself to be deceived by the raw emotions found at the root of militancy's disciplined enthusiasm knows full well that the need to forget and the industry of forgetting establish dynamics more powerful than the fragile vitality of memories that resist. In Gelman's poem, the proclamation is made through a coarse dialogue, or perhaps a disjointed quarrel, between three dissimilar voices. In this rebuke between a first person weeping and feeling sorry for himself, a second person reminding him that there is also sweetness and encouraging him to recapture it, and a third person who asks for resistance, to whom should we listen? Is it possible to take into account all three voices at the same time? If so, then what notion emerges of a first person who resists?

For now, both moral and political resistance—those two beacons of hope—appear to be a necessity under certain circumstances. What is more, part of the experience through which the human animal learns to construct itself includes saying no, fully aware of the serious consequences that this "no" can bring. Unfortunately, there is no school where one can attend classes in "theories of resistance," receiving precise instructions that can later be applied when necessary. Only in the overcrowded and slightly chaotic "school of life" do we learn the virtues involved in reacting in opposition to something.

Gelman's more recent poems, all written in lowercase letters—perhaps trying to make as little noise as possible—continue to focus on these anxieties. The poem "elsewhere" ["otras partes"] seems to challenge us to keep up the fight despite our frustration and disappointment. Although the rallying cries alluded to are both local and nominal, almost imperceptible, they do not represent a lesser form of resistance:

did you here/ my love?/ we're leaving
bearing the defeat elsewhere/

10 "Ir y quedarse, y con quedar, partirse; / Partir sin alma, y ir con alma ajena."

bearing this animal elsewhere/
the dead elsewhere/[11]

The dead remain present, a terrible burden that is so difficult to leave behind yet impossible to bear. Sometimes they become embedded, neither leaving nor conceding. Of course, the deaths that weigh the most are those that only happened just yesterday. However, on occasions we not only have to bear immediate deaths, but also the almost invisible deaths of a *present past*—that is, those deaths that could not be laid to rest and, thus, continue to haunt us. They are grieving souls asking that we grant them a place in our memory. In *Com/positions* (1984–1985) [*Com/posiciones* (1984–1985)], Gelman succeeds in lending his words to those spirits (perhaps distant mirrors tormenting us with their reproaches, interrogations and lessons). Solomon Ibn Gabirol (1021–1055), known as the Jewish Plato, speaks through Gelman's words to remember a deterioration process that often occurs during exile, especially when it is lived as absolute loss:

at this midnight hour in exile
I am myself a beast/[12]

However, the words that Gelman attributes to the Jewish rationalist Yehuda Al-harizi (1170–1237), translator of the works of Maimonides, magically return us to Alberti's affirmative tone:

they banished me from my land/
I walked throughout the land/
they expelled me from my language/
it came along with me[13]

For his part, the philosopher Yehuda Halevi (1075–1141) warns us that we should not overlook how exile is usually accompanied by an internal exile: an exile from love.

until I find my way to you/
my bones tremble holding up a stranger/[14]

---

11 "¿oíste/ corazón/ nos vamos / con la derrota a otra parte/ / con este animal a otra parte/ / los muertos a otra parte/"

12 "en esta medianoche del exilio / soy yo mismo una bestia/"

13 "me desterraron de mi tierra/ / caminé por la tierra/ / me deportaron de mi lengua/ / ella me acompañó"

14 "mientras no encuentre mi camino hacia vos/ / mis huesos tiemblan sosteniendo a un extraño/"

All of these words also contain a Stoic warning: no one has the right to cause anyone else to be unhappy. Not even devastating pain can grant that right. On the contrary, with each step we can and should push aside our suffering for the purpose of resisting. There is no excuse not to find bridges that will show us the way across the abyss. Therefore, when exile is lived as resistance, not only as loss, poems cease to be testaments and become proclamations.

Proclamation: a public notification so that a matter of great importance can be made known to everyone. A speech or address given aloud or in written form. A rallying cry directed at an audience to explain the goals of the person voicing it and what those listening should do.

Those who witness horrific events and the proclamations they make afterwards possess a moral value deserving of our trust and respect—perhaps also of our gratitude. Being a witness to suffering and abuse is a serious matter, which explains the severity with which perjurers are judged and condemned in these cases. But let us not forget that just like testament-poems, proclamation-poems also represent *meta*-testimonies: samples of anomalous speech. Unlike life stories, interviews, autobiographies, identity narratives, private letters and personal memories, poems are metatestimonies that are understood using a reader's sensitivity and imagination. It follows that the guarantor of these proclamations *is not* and *cannot be* the authority of the first person, as is the case in testimonies of injustice.

I argue that according to practical knowledge of the rhetorical tradition, verse is used not only to revive the remnants of an experience, but also to elaborate it without excluding the help of fiction. Because of the distance created in such transformations, we can ask these metatestimonies (where exile is expressed as resistance) certain upsetting questions regarding the limitations of all types of resisting. Let us not forget that the *principle of presumed trust* is precisely that: a presumption. A presumption is a belief that I hold onto until presented with doubts or reasons against it. Therefore, at the first sign of arrogant reasoning operating inside the way we are living exile as resistance, would it not be prudent to exercise the art of self-interruption, distrusting the self who resists and instead turn our attention elsewhere? In our moral and political behavior, should we be content with only resisting? At some point should we not attempt to move on from resistance, however justified that resistance may be?

These questions might seem excessive if we overlook the first property that characterizes the action of resisting: behavior that is partly reactive and partly active. Consider the first element of this property: "partly reactive." When resisting a given situation there is no acceptance of it, but there is also no separation from it. What does this mean? Let us listen to the voice of another woman who, facing tragedy, abandons the first-person point of view so as not to fall prey to the *principle of general credulity*. Inside this detour, there lies a proclamation that resonates: we must be cautious. Sometimes conceiving exile as resistance can also result in one finding excuses during a tragedy—tragedies like exile—to revel in letting oneself die.

On that subject, the Uruguayan Cristina Peri Rossi formulates an intricate allegory in her *Description of a Shipwreck* [*Descripción de un naufragio*]. Every allegory creates a fictional tale that opens up the possibility for multiple interpretations. In this example, Peri Rossi sets masculine and feminine perspectives against one another. Of course, the expressions "masculine perspective" and "feminine perspective" denote social constructions connected to a historical moment. In this particular case, they refer to a long-standing tradition with various layers of deeply-ingrained stereotypes: active versus passive, public versus private, warrior versus peacemaker, defiance versus complacence or that opposition found in Ida Vitale's poem: clarity versus passion.

Notice that the masculine perspective finds itself caught up inside an unusual act of pride. This pride is "unusual" because here the heroic gesture is nothing more than a sacrifice. It *wants* to embrace defeat—perhaps gloriously, but for whom?

> At the cry of "Save yourselves"
> everyone jumped into the boats
> almost everyone, except me.[15]

The masculine self informs, "I could have saved myself and I didn't. I resisted." One might ask why the masculine voice chose not to accept the risk of saving himself. Could it be because it would have meant the purest form of selfishness, a characteristic incompatible with the conduct exemplified by a warrior? Or did he opt not to pay that price because he considered it to be too cheap? Or is it more likely that the contradictory demands of masculine subjectivity forced him to accept the comfort of remaining huddled in place: yet another victim taking pleasure in their fate? Instead of dismissing these doubts, the voice formulated as the "masculine perspective" utters, "Here is my testament. I was there, and I heroically decided to let myself die." At the same time, he disapprovingly notices the dramatic actions taken by the woman. She wants to save herself too quickly, without hesitation, with no consideration for the standards of dignity. This social construction of the masculine gaze considers with disdain, or more likely with envy, her fierce embrace of self-responsibility: the incessant act of transforming hands, arms, legs into wings that can carry

15 "Al grito de "Sálvese quien pueda" / todo el mundo se echó a los botes, / casi todos, menos yo."

you to safety. But to where? Anywhere. It matters not. In times of tragedy, what is most important is that you stay above water, despite everything else.

Leaving no doubt that he has decided to let himself drown, the man's voice confirms the scene in which the woman inconsiderately, fearlessly pushes forward.

> with that tremendous instinct possessed by mothers
> and survivors.
> In catastrophes only the strongest survive.[16]

Thus, the woman's departure is described as a variation of another social construction born of masculine resentment: "women can be extremely brutal when they choose to be." However, the decisiveness and even ruthlessness that the "masculine perspective" attaches to this woman's behavior is soon revealed to be nothing more than his own projection, perhaps out of fear, perhaps out of envy or perhaps a mixture of both emotions. When it is the woman's turn to speak, her words redescribe the scene. She confesses that if she had indeed so unabashedly thrown herself into the sea, it was because at that moment "resisting" meant "to die."

And just like that, leaving behind that terrible period in which she flailed between life and death, the feminine voice decides to jump as if she had been waiting for:

> the ultimate moment of solitude
> when nothing matters
> nothing else remains
> but the undeniable desire to live.[17]

"It is not I who is hostile and cruel, rather the circumstances and history in general," the woman's voice seems to confirm as she accepts her solitude. It is true that she makes no more attempts to resist. She wants only to survive. It is easy to understand that if she had taken just one moment to register her situation, if she had paused even briefly to consider the facts of the matter and what she was leaving behind, tragedy might have taken her life. In this sense, the woman inverts the values found in the tradition of exile as loss, as well as those in the tradition of exile as resistance. The description of them she provides differs

16 "con el tremendo instinto de las madres / y de los sobrevivientes. / De las catástrofes perduran los más fuertes."

17 "el momento supremo de soledad / en que nada pesa / nada queda ya / sino el deseo impostergable de vivir."

from that of the "masculine perspective" since even in his struggle against outside impositions—the definition of resistance—he accepts at least some of their rules as a starting point. Contrary to that slight acceptance, however limited it may be, this allegory presents another form of behavior: one must know when to break with the resistance's reactive component and heed the sometimes almost superhuman impulses to leave. What matters is starting a new story, even if it means bearing the burden of defeat.

It also highlights the fact that this is the only possible option if one is to choose life, in further opposition to the heroically masculine perspective of resistance. Consequently, somewhere between the poem's verses there appear to be various reproaches levied against the masculine "you." Reproaches such as: "You did not sacrifice yourself, you let yourself die, proof that you did not love me enough to fight and come with me." Or put even more simply: "You gave up. You took shelter inside the shipwreck, proof that you did not love life enough." And we are again faced with that awful, but categorical, choice in which there is no longer any place for resistance. The only options are either to stay and die or, standing there on the precipice, hard-hearted and with closed eyes, assume the terrible strength needed to leave without goodbyes in pursuit of a new horizon. Through our continued experimentation with certain verses, we have, little by little, reached a second type of exile's direct lessons.

There Is a Time to Resist and a Time to Break with the Situation Being Resisted as Well as with Resistance Itself

Like exile's first type of direct lessons, this second type is also precarious given the tension between these two completely divergent mindsets. And again, in order for one attitude not to ruin the other, they must be set against one another. Certainly, it is our responsibility not to surrender and to fight, to the extent possible, to recover what has been taken from us. Or in more definitive words, we have the responsibility to learn to resist. When resistance means standing up to injustice, inaction is not an option. Traditionally, every social order teaches us to submit to the prevailing norms, even if they are unjust. This is why it is critical to promote a culture that does not neglect the "raw material of indignation." Otherwise, fear will begin to invade our lives, growing inside our cities, our houses and even our beds. And this will sooner or later lead to a nervous blindness or to its counterpart, indifference, which ultimately results in self-destruction.

Out of moral and political responsibility, we rescue certain behaviors such as resisting or bearing testimony to miseries, disasters and exterminations. However, they soon lose their value and risk becoming excessively deceptive glorifications. Or worse still, when the demands of a resisting subjectivity emerge, if it does not accept its limits, does it not undermine these behaviors or rid them of their value altogether by trapping them inside its arrogant reasoning?

Let us examine the color of expressions like "this action only possesses testimonial value" that accompany certain hypocritical behaviors. While resistance is publicly and resoundingly praised, other voices mumble in not-so-soft whispers that such actions lack both political and moral effectiveness. In this whispering, the so-called "testimonial value" is reduced to one of those faint sentimental decorations that Hegel characterized as belonging to "beautiful souls." In the long run, is this what unruly industry will do with such noble beginnings: normalize the voice of a dissenting subjectivity with respect to a social system and its insatiable interference? Should not the recent boom in the industry of memory and resistance testimonies, like any overly-lauded success, be cause for alarm and suspicion?

Another question, even more alarming and likely to be dismissed as an affront: would it not be wise for the diverse political ideas used to formulate resistance, as convincing as they might be, to also include momentary interruptions, brief moments of fracturing? After all, these are reactive behaviors determined in part by certain demands. We should remember that all resistance is governed by a disturbing dependence on past and present suffering. These ties are aggressive, sometimes engaging in open combat, yet they are still ties that bind. There is, of course, a bond that is much worse—worse because it is much stronger—which forms between one's hatred and what one hates. Anyone who easily hates also becomes obsessed, even intoxicated, by certain aspects of what they are hating. Unfortunately, the resistance mindset contains and develops hatred, albeit usually with good reason. It is perhaps even necessary. However, the ties between the action of resistance and what is being resisted, or between hatred and what is being hated, are soon found to be examples of a disturbing and far-reaching behavioral pattern: *the paradox of practices that, while rejecting, incessantly reproduce what they reject.*

How does this work? Hate tends to eternalize its object. Does resistance not do the same thing? Actions like disrupting, expressing outrage, disobeying, contradicting or tearfully protesting also become caught up in this paradox. For example, creating a disruption involves employing exaggerated behavior against what is popularly (and deceptively) considered to be correct within a society or group. As with any exaggerated act, one wants to attract attention—to point out the true repressive nature of accepted "good" policies, "good" habits, etc. However, a disruption represents only an isolated and, most of all, transitory measure. If this were not the case, it would soon lose its effectiveness (faster than the tears we shed in protest could dry). Or even worse, the disruption could be effective and, as a result, be assimilated into convention—"co-opted," as they say—or it could be defeated, which would help to strengthen those conventions that gave rise to the disruption in the first place. Why not insist, then, on exercising good judgment in order to identify the limitations inherent in any practice of strictly oppositional behavior? Rather than honor, or what is easily mistaken as such, is it not time that we restore the value of actions where one leaves for another place, without goodbyes?

If the answer is "yes," then within the notions of self that emerge from this second type of exile lesson, just like with the first type, we will have to integrate conflicting practices. We will still heed the maxim "One must learn to resist," but we will also allow for moments of cautious distancing, even (with anxiety and guilt) retreating, while weeping in protest, "I know what I'm talking about because I was there, I lived it, I suffered it in flesh and blood and that is why I will never be able to stop resisting them." We will also keep a respectful distance from assertions like: "These wounds cannot be healed because they belong to that nonnegotiable and irremediable order of the Incurable, which is also the ultimate order of Justice." Of course, there are wounds that are incurable and many atrocities that belong to the order of the Nonnegotiable.

Nevertheless, for strategic or practical purposes, since it is impossible to imprison an entire society or even a significantly large part of it, one will have to neglect feelings of rage, that persistent rage—during times of so-called "democratic transitions," for example—that comes from having to continue to share a common space with the oppressors and many of their accomplices. Therefore, in the years following social catastrophes, of which exile is a consequence, national politics will have to manage the impossible, cure the incurable, negotiate the nonnegotiable. But there are certainly reasons to negotiate the nonnegotiable *that go beyond all strategy and all practicality*, provided we do not lose sight of what we are doing. In that delicate management of the impossible, the victims' desire to live in freedom must also be honored, furthering their initial effort to build a morally-inhabitable future. Additionally, the deplorable motto "Let justice be done even if the world perishes" meticulously conceals its delusional reasoning. It is not only bad advice, but also sets a trap for us because if the world perishes, then nothing matters anymore anyway.

Keeping in mind (sometimes with great frustration) *the paradox of practices that, while rejecting, incessantly reproduce what they reject*, we must eliminate the physical applications of the word "resist" to the movement of power within social life, those which lead to the determination that "x pressure equals x resistance." There are moments when it is worth exploring the possibility of an escape from this reactive behavior and its "x pressure equals x resistance" calculations so as to preserve only the second property in the concept of resistance: its courage, in the form of the determination and intense desire to start over. This does not prevent us from acknowledging that learning to resist is a good lesson in courage. We should also note that, varying this tradition's stereotypes regarding masculine and feminine, we must move away from the socially-constructed "masculine courage"—which squanders its universally touted heroism in pursuit of absolutes—and toward the often silent but firm "feminine courage"—which accepts what is unavoidable during the next few months, the next few years or the next few minutes.

In summary, according to this second lesson of exile, we should use the materials of suffering to generate a force that will work in opposition to what has caused or continues to cause it. However, in order to accomplish this, we must look to that "feminine courage"—all too familiar with ruptures—so that we can subvert the entire situation in which the injustice has occurred, or continues to occur, disregarding many interventions from the past. It means again carrying out complex and risky practices to place the experiences of resistance and the evils being resisted upon a single, shared horizon. This horizon will contain everything and much more because rarely should we allow ourselves the luxury of forgetting that the world is (much) greater than that which we are resisting or disrupting, even when there are moral and political reasons that justify us doing so. It then becomes possible to escape the obsessions that often arise in exile, and during forced displacements in general, by making the difficult and sometimes horrifying resolution to transform courageousness into the will to leave in search of other desires, other notions of self, other emotions, other arguments and other tasks.

CHAPTER 5

Exile as a New Beginning

Many Spanish intellectuals who were forced to leave after the defeat of the Republic in 1939 used the word "transterrado" to characterize their situation in Mexico, where they felt that they were in a land that was an extension of their own. We can assume that these exiles suffered greatly as they bid farewell to their commitments, their professions, their loves, their books and their surroundings. Even so, the hardworking days they spent in Mexico seem to confirm that this forced displacement brought out the strength for them to realize that they could resume their jobs, their writings and their projects. One who lives in exile as a "transterrado" does not lose sight of what they have lost. At the same time, they know or have a sense that there is another life to be gained by exercising their ability to remember and to forget. On occasion, unfortunate circumstances can force one to discover unexpectedly admirable ways of carrying out the human task. The territories that we consider to be our own expand. Even under the worst circumstances one can sometimes spot the possibility of wiping the slate clean and starting anew.

In this sense, exile not only opens horrible, compulsory exit doors—as many biblical texts have shown—but also entry doors: thresholds to new experiences and, perhaps, lessons to be learned. Predictably, someone living as a "transterrado" rejects the image of the exile produced by traditions of loss or of resistance. A "transterrado" is neither a socially incapacitated person improvising testaments, nor a rebel in distant lands resisting and dictating proclamations. Through raging force of will, a "transterrado" ignores borders because they have decided to take up residence inside the various registers of their language and in the diverse regions of this foreign world that belongs equally to us all—as many, including the Cynics and Stoics, have shown. This is the aspiration (or perhaps the delusion) that we can regain from cosmopolitan thinking. For the sake of continuing our investigation, let us assume that, with regards to these experiences, we are not delusional, or at least not completely.

Thus, living exile as a new beginning involves breaking with the usual path of desires, beliefs, emotions and expectations by transforming the experiences of exile into an entryway to other possibilities; this is its first property. The second property of exile as a new beginning is that one must attempt to make this rupture a permanent, institutionalized way of life.

Apart from notorious prophets of Israel and their outrageous predictions, what metatestimonies can we find where exile is experienced as a new

 | DOI:10.1163/9789004385153_007

beginning? It is not without some hesitation that I now consider the difficult and, without a doubt, highly debatable case of what we might describe as Luis Cernuda's negative cosmopolitanism. Like the Cynics, many times Cernuda might have professed: "I am a foreigner in every land." One might immediately, and alarmingly, object, "What can Cernuda, of all people, have to do with living exile as a new beginning?"

Initially, through his bitter and often violent fortitude, his words attempt to distance themselves as much as possible from the tradition of exile as loss where one's longing shuts out the rest of the world. The following verses from the poem "Spanish Diptych" ["Díptico español"], published in one of his last books of poetry *Desolation of the Chimera* [*Desolación de la quimera*]—or, the last section of his complete works *Reality and Desire* [*La realidad y el deseo*]—lay bare the "raw material of indignation":

> What man's spirit
> Has achieved for the good of man's spirit
> Throughout the centuries,
> Is our patrimony and the inheritance
> Of future men.
> By allowing them to deny
> And steal this from us, man then descends,
> –How far?– down that rigid scale
> That rises from animals up to man.[1]

We again find the "rigid scale" that appeared in the verses of Pedro Garfias' *Spring in Eaton Hastings*, a poem which was a part of the tradition of exile that is experienced only as loss and where, in the solitude brought on by exile, those around us become vegetables and minerals. However, Cernuda's poem counters this by arguing that when such a situation occurs, our own position on the scale of living things lowers: we weaken ourselves, we become lost, we disappear. This is another way of suggesting that if we remain inside the tradition of exile as loss, we will eventually bring about our own annihilation. By sliding backwards in evolution, the human animal loses its human component.

Still, it would be difficult for this metatestimony to incorporate the tradition of exile as resistance, in the more or less political sense of the word.

1 "Lo que el espíritu del hombre / Ganó para el espíritu del hombre / A través de los siglos, / Es patrimonio nuestro y es herencia / De los hombres futuros. / Al tolerar que nos lo nieguen / Y secuestren, el hombre entonces baja, / ¿Y cuánto?, en esa escala dura / Que desde el animal llega hasta el hombre."

In Cernuda's poem we find verses that could have been written by Aristippus or other Cynics of ancient times. Exile teaches resistance. Nevertheless, resisting various social identifications and counteridentifications is only one important step in not allowing oneself to be overcome, as we saw in alternative Socratism:

> I am halfheartedly Spanish
> Living as best I can so far away from my land[2]

Again, like the Cynics and the Stoics, Cernuda knows full well that there is no reason why we should definitively divide up human events since we are all members of humanity. Each human life is a part of other "wholes":

> The same language that they spoke before,
> And well before we were born,
> The peoples in whom our experience finds roots.[3]

No person begins from zero. Every beginning occurs amid an inheritance. *Amid*: we are born amid other people who are in some way part of a society, of a culture. We begin to speak using the voices that we have inherited. Still, the reality that our determination to begin necessarily takes place "amid" does not imply that it is any less of a new beginning, of a "being at the threshold" situation. No person:

> chooses their tradition, or their homeland,
> Or their language either; they serve them,
> Devotedly if possible.
> But the greatest devotion
> Is to their conscience; and that is what I serve[4]

Awareness is a threshold. The first person, armed with the possibility of reflection and able to assume the distance that this allows, can now question their social identifications and counteridentifications. In doing so, they can break with many diverse affiliations: with family, with language, with cultural traditions, with fellow citizens. This removes any pretension to essentiality

2 "Soy español sin ganas / Que vive como puede bien lejos de su tierra"

3 "La misma lengua con que hablaron antes, / Y mucho antes de nacer nosotros, / Las gentes en que hallara raíz nuestra experiencia."

4 "su tradición escoge, ni su tierra, / Ni tampoco su lengua; a ellas sirve, / Fielmente si es posible. / Mas la fidelidad más alta / Es para su conciencia; y yo a ésa sirvo"

and absoluteness from their systems of belonging. When one is loyal to one's conscience, there is no longer exclusive mention made of these appointed positions now that the system's disturbing eventualities have been exposed. Relying only on itself for a moment, the first person speaks from a space of "human free will"—to borrow an expression from Cernuda—the perspective of the "everyman."

But Cernuda not only formulates thresholds in thought through which identifications and counteridentifications can be challenged for the purpose of preserving certain ones and rejecting others. He also believes that new beginnings are possible by recovering the experience of the body, its feelings and its desires. For this, let us look at the poem "The date" ["La fecha"]—which, it seems, was written on the author's birthday and contradicts the title of the collection in which it is included: *Living Without Being Alive* [*Vivir sin estar viviendo*]. It makes it clear that the voice speaking finds itself in exile:

> Also under strange skies
> And in a strange region[5]

The poem repeatedly states that he is a foreigner, a guest. It adds, however, that this is inconsequential because inside every sunrise lies the possibility of a threshold of flowers, of skies, of seas:

> At the threshold hydrangeas
> With clear skies, then
> The sea, without memory[6]

In these words, we find oppositions characteristic of a search for a new beginning: surrounding oneself with happy, lighthearted presences like hydrangeas, clear skies and the sea rather than one's memory and the spiraling *present past*, that unwanted inheritance of so many burdensome absences. We cannot help but ask how we might prepare ourselves to break free of the losses that overwhelm us and the resistances that blind us? We can find an answer to this in the perspective that teaches us that in any situation there are always multiple doors to choose from and never only one. I suspect that one must necessarily be receptive, maybe even irresponsibly so, in order to approach any "being at the threshold" situation as a chance at a new beginning:

---

5 "También en cielo extraño / Y en extraña comarca"

6 "En el umbral hortensias / Con cielo claro, luego / El mar, sin la memoria"

Over there are the roads,
In this light, still
Empty, and among them
One awaits your departure.[7]

A person starting anew is encouraged to forget ever so slightly their ability to reason. Sometimes one must give in to what the body demands, to the unexpected enjoyment of the road. Consequently, the first person almost inevitably tries not to be unkind to itself when coming across a threshold:

Do not ask if it is worth
The trouble to have come,
But let go, think
That a god is today your friend.[8]

What "god" can he be referring to that could be a "friend" today in exile? Those pagan gods are, for Cernuda, the bodies of his young lovers. In some instances, embracing a body makes it possible to erase all tragedy. In Poem X titled "With you" ["Contigo"] from his *Poems for a Body* [*Poemas para un cuerpo*]—which, according to Cernuda in *History of a Book* [*Historial de un libro*], expresses (i.e., reconstructs and meditates on) his intense relationship with the Mexican boxer Salvador Alighieri—redemption is all-encompassing. When one person is with the other, there is no more exile; not even death is possible. Embracing the other's body is to embrace all lands, all life:

Exile and death
Are for me where
You are not.[9]

If we were cautiously hesitant about approaching Cernuda's verses as potential metatestimonies of living exile as a new beginning, then Juan Ramón Jiménez's final poems will certainly be even less-likely candidates for metatestimonies of… well, of anything whatsoever. After so many years dedicated to writing with such admirable clarity—or rather with such admirable freshness that his words are suspended almost miraculously in midair—his exile poems

7 "Allá están los caminos, / A esta luz todavía / Vacíos, y entre ellos / Uno aguarda tu ida."
8 "No preguntes si vale / La pena haber venido, / Sino déjate, piensa / Que un dios es hoy tu amigo."
9 "El destierro y la muerte / Para mí están adonde / No estés tú."

still continue to baffle readers. "Space" ["Espacio"], a long prose poem written toward the end of his life (and composed over more than ten years, between 1941 and 1954), consists of three stanzas or fragments with words seemingly connected only by their rhythm and a new discovery at every turn. Images and thoughts flow in every direction, which makes it difficult for us to read only some of its words here, knowing that so many others are being lost. Nevertheless, I am obligated to do so. Somewhat arbitrarily, let us look at several strange words from the first fragment:

> I am not present only, but an escaping torrent from beginning to end... In the middle there is, there has to be a point, an exit... And the language, what confusion! what is it we tell ourselves without knowing what we are telling ourselves... What fact of life, with its farce, judges death without facts and imprisons it in impotence? Yes, all, all has been more, and all will be more! It is not the present, but instead a point of support or of comparison, shorter each time; and what it leaves and what it takes, more, greater. No, that dog barking at the setting sun is not barking in Monturrio in Moguer, or near Carmona in Sevilla, or on Torrijos Street in Madrid; it is barking in Miami, Coral Gables, Florida, and I am hearing it there, there, not here, not here, there, there. How fiercely the dog always barks at the sun in full flight![10]

Good sense teaches us that a confession lightens the soul. I confess that I hardly understand what is happening with the many words in "Space" aside from a personal suspicion that they are alluding to ways of identifying thresholds for new beginnings. How do the words connect to one another? What do these words mean? Or better yet, what are they attempting to do with their readers? What experiments do they have in mind for our desires? What notions of self are they trying to convey to us? Sometimes a detailed examination of "what thing we are telling ourselves without knowing what we are telling ourselves"

10 "No soy presente solo, sino fuga raudal de cabo a fin... En medio hay, tiene que haber un punto, una salida... Y el idioma, ¡qué confusión!, qué cosa nos decimos sin saber lo que nos decimos... ¿Qué ley de vida juzga con su farsa a la muerte sin ley y la aprisiona en la impotencia? ¡Sí, todo, todo ha sido más y todo será más! No es el presente sino un punto de apoyo o de comparación, más breve cada vez; y lo que deja y lo que coje, más, más grande. No, ese perro que ladra al sol caído, no ladra en el Monturrio de Moguer, ni cerca de Carmona de Sevilla, ni en la calle Torrijos de Madrid; ladra en Miami, Coral Gables, La Florida, y yo lo estoy oyendo allí, allí, no aquí, no aquí, allí, allí. ¡Qué vivo ladra siempre el perro al sol que huye!"

leads us to experiment with what we hardly understand or with what we do not understand at all. But let us move slowly.

I will make several (very) tentative observations in a small attempt to approach some of my confusion concerning these initial words. The first words of the fragment (the first verse?) are perhaps implicitly stating: "Unfortunately I am not only being present. I am also fleeing." And maybe this artifact is dramatizing the conflict between the realization that we only live in the present—in the moment—and that which is bringing the present to an end: the "escaping torrent," the "sun in full flight," the days of those stories and plans when "all has been more, and all will be more." Among these strange words, "more" is a relative term and "all" is a determiner whose unverifiability is troublesome, save when it refers to a designated group. How is it that "all" can have been and will be "more"? Might it involve that awful nightmare where the past and the future are "more" than the present? Regardless, does this prose poem not suggest that there must be a way out of that delusion? For example, perhaps by realizing that an authentic point of support, or of comparison, can only be found in the present. Are these words alluding to a sort of rupture in that "escaping torrent"? Then, should every present be lived as if it were a threshold that breaches the "escaping torrent"? If so, then this threshold is more fleeting but denser than we would like to believe. Through reflection we can admit that the present is more fleeting than we imagine, although it paradoxically holds more: it contains itself as well as the enormous past and the no less enormous future. Does each and every present encapsulate the entirety of life? Is it not necessary that the here and now be allowed to become a part of that incessant flow? Does the present exist as overlapping time periods and, simultaneously, as a rupture? At every turn, are there exits leading to a particular present: exits that we often try to ignore?

From the poem's second fragment I will only include the beginning where the connections between moments in time are again emphasized. Like the Stoics (but with a somewhat nomadic Stoicism if this is not an oxymoron), Juan Ramón Jiménez might have professed: "My home is in all lands. I inhabit the world."

> "And for me to remember why I have lived," I come here to you, Hudson River of my sea. "Love was sweet like this light… And under Washington Bridge (the greatest bridge in this New York) flow the yellow fields of my childhood." Childhood, I am a boy again and I am, lost, so old, in vastness. Unforeseen folklore: "love is sweet like the light," and this New York is just like Moguer, it is just like Sevilla and Madrid. The wind at the corner of Broadway, just like at Pneumonia Corner on my own Rascón Street, can

> carry me away; and I have the door open where I live, with sun shining in.[11]

Does the expression "I have the door open where I live, with sun shining in" describe a certain present and, as such, move us closer to situations of "being at the threshold"? The burden of some present moments seems to span all other times and spaces. The overflowing density above does not perceive differences: New York is the same as Moguer. Outside, the sun flees. Inside, the same sun stays. Seneca already showed us that Rome and Corsica are basically the same city because they lie beneath the same sun. Therefore, does exile matter at all?

The third fragment vaguely alludes to his specific exile with details of a horrible scene, perhaps the remains of a memory: "not even the filthy scrap of paper, square and indigo, a complaint in pencil, against me, Madrid at war."[12] And let us look at yet another strange passage appearing almost at the end.

> My body does not envy you, consciousness, but it hopes that when you leave, you will take it with you, and that you will give it, when giving yourself to whomever, all it deserves, this love that it has given to you so unique, so alone, as great as what is unique and what is alone.[13]

Does the writing here—the syntax, in particular—not achieve the symbolic translation of a flowing movement: a river or an ocean? Or maybe an escape along with a reconciliation during that very same escape? Like in Cernuda, but in a very different way, it would appear that consciousness manages to merge with the body. When both leave, is love "what is unique and what is alone"? At this point I will conclude (possibly too quickly) my attempt to experiment with "Space." While reading and rereading I was reminded a little of those dreams where one moment you believe that you understand clearly how one event connects with the others only to suddenly have the sensation that a train is rushing

11 "'Y para recordar por qué he vivido,' vengo a ti, río Hudson de mi mar. 'Dulce como esta luz era el amor… Y por debajo de Washington Bridge (el puente más con más de esta New York) pasa el campo amarillo de mi infancia.' Infancia, niño vuelvo a ser y soy, perdido, tan mayor, en lo más grande. Leyenda inesperada: "dulce como la luz es el amor," y esta New York es igual que Moguer, es igual que Sevilla y que Madrid. Puede el viento, en la esquina de Broadway, como en la esquina de las Pulmonías de mi calle Rascón, conmigo; y tengo abierta la puerta donde vivo, con sol dentro."

12 "ni el papelito sucio, cuadradillo añil, de la denuncia a lápiz, contra mí, Madrid en guerra."

13 "Mi cuerpo no se encela de ti, conciencia, mas quisiera que al irte fueras todo él, y que dieras a él, al darte tú a quien sea, lo suyo todo, este amar que te ha dado tan único, tan solo, tan grande como lo único y lo solo."

towards you, crossing a field at high speed and then quickly disappearing over the horizon, leaving faint signals behind that are increasingly difficult to distinguish. From the remains of those signals, this reading hopes to rescue two possible ideas regarding the meaning of "new beginning" situations in exile.

In "Space," I have (maybe only) learned that being at a threshold implies, above all, embracing that brief, extremely dense time that fills every present moment. However, when confronting this wall of words, almost at the limit of meaning, and attempting to make sense of it, I also find that a "being at a threshold" situation can arise from the desire to understand and not being able to or the desire to understand and understanding something without being sure what has been understood: the desire to understand, not understanding, but without ceasing to try to understand. For if one stops trying to understand when not understanding, then not understanding is no longer a luminous boundary—luminous in the sense that it relates or suggests possible relations between both sides of the boundary—but rather a false door where you let yourself be deceived.

I want to linger on this subject just a bit longer with the following metatestimony from the Chilean Gonzalo Rojas where putting words on display becomes a celebration. Its title reminds us, consciously or not, of the Spanish exile in Mexico:

Transtierro

1

I look at the air in the air, these years
will pass so many with dust-filled wind
beneath the eyelid so many
in exile.

2

I will eat earth
from the Earth under slabs
of cement, I will become an eye,
surging waves I will become.[14]

In this metatestimony, air takes the place of the sun that appears in other exile poems. Air is in all places. Air is common to all women and all men alike. Exile

14 "*Transtierro*: 1 // Miro el aire en el aire, pasarán / estos años cuántos de viento sucio / debajo del párpado cuántos / del exilio. // 2 // comeré tierra / de la Tierra bajo las tablas / del cemento, me haré ojo, / oleaje me haré."

can take away a great many things, but not the sun and not the air. There are, however, many categories of air: good air, bad air. Dust-filled wind is bad air. But is should be accommodated. It must receive its place among the other types of air. The dust-filled wind is only temporary. We must live with this expectation or else fall prey to a life of exile experienced only as loss.

When we close our eyes, they are covered by our eyelids. The dust-filled wind and the closed eyelid can be read as representations of a person in exile. Still, we must wager that the dusty wind will move on, and the exiled person will open their eyes. In the poem, they will become an eye, not a closed eyelid. And according to these verses not just an eye, but an eye in movement: an eye transformed into waves (perhaps Cernuda's sea without memory?). Rojas' metatestimony continues:

> 3
> standing
> upon the rock of identity, this
> bone and no other I will become, this
> corneal music of mine.
>
> 4
> through an opening.
> Leaving
> I am, leaving I will be.
> Leaving, leaving, leaving.[15]

Do I exist because I have been identified? Does that identification correspond to my culture? But is the culture I inhabit not riddled with eventualities? Similar to Cernuda's poems, the first person seems to be able to break with systems of belonging by becoming the contemplative eye and surging waves. All that remains is its intense will pronouncing the word "*parto*" and its double meaning, lost in its English translation: *partir* (to leave), *parir* (to be born).

I am leaving, because exile has taken my home from me. But in Spanish "*parto*" also means "birth." When making a "being at the threshold" situation out of the act of leaving (often kicking and screaming), by turning to the art of self-interruption, this act of leaving can be understood as an act being born: I am leaving towards what I will become, towards what I can create even under adverse conditions. In exile, must I then be my own midwife?

15 "3 // parado / en la roca de la identidad, este / hueso y no otro me haré, esta / música mía córnea. // 4 // por hueca. / Parto / soy, parto seré. / Parto, parto, parto."

As another experiment, it is possible to read Rojas' metatestimony by contrasting the actions of leaving and fleeing—keeping in mind the alternative socratism of Aristippus and the Cynics. Should we be willing to leave others and ourselves, but without fleeing the world? Undoubtedly, numerous "being at the threshold" situations will sometimes advise us to leave, but to avoid fleeing like a criminal who staggers hesitantly forward, fearing their own destruction inside an increasingly foreign world.

Based on these readings, I propose five observations to assist with new beginnings:

- *New beginnings as awareness.* Recognizing and, most of all, reflecting on the role played by the social identifications and counteridentifications that define us, and then evaluating them, requires that we step away—even if we must employ certain devices to do so. In this way, we are able to at least question the validity of the credentials bestowed upon us by various systems of belonging (a State, a family, a corporation…).
- *New beginnings as accepting the body's wisdom.* Sometimes only the necessities and limits of the body, and even the non-theoretical content of its experiences, can clear away the illusions and allow us to reach solid ground. There are situations in which the most instinctive reactions, for example, physical pleasure or disgust, are all that a person has left.
- *New beginnings as embracing the present.* Existence frequently occurs amid memories and plans for the future without realizing that those memories and plans can take place nowhere else but in the here and now. It bears repeating: only the neglected and often-wasted present exists, "with sun shining in."
- *New beginnings as a struggle for understanding.* Familiarity persuades us to consider only what is a part of our deep-seated perspectives and it leaves us blind and deaf to everything else. This is why when I do not understand immediately, I often turn to my arrogant reasoning and declare: "this is unintelligible." On rare occasions, if that "I" can forget itself for just a short time and make the effort to understand the thing that is resisting being understood, if arrogant reasoning or exhaustion does not win out, then perhaps it will discover new lessons, both direct and indirect.
- *New beginnings as departing toward self-reinvention.* With respect to imposed actions such as exile, the most common reaction is to curl up inside the sense of loss or, with some effort, to learn to resist. However, by partially breaking with the demands of the past and the present, one can also risk being an agent and initiate new courses of action; this is what is promised by the most dreaded and daring use of the word "freedom."

If we at least keep these possible ideas regarding new-beginning actions in mind, it will not be surprising when the metatestimonies generated during an exile that is experienced this way are no longer testaments (like during exile as loss) or proclamations (like during exile as resistance), but instead become incantations. What do I mean by this?

Incantation: the use of words that have been granted extraordinary qualities. An urgent appeal or invocation carried out in order to ward off evil or bad luck when starting an adventure and hoping to ward off failure or curses. Emphatic prayers.

What evils are these incantation poems seeking to deter? They are attempting to break the curse of paralyzing illusions and blinding familiarities. At the very least, they are encouraging self-interruption: a pause from those desires, beliefs, emotions and expectations that unceasingly identify, counter-identify and, as a result, prioritize seemingly irrefutable tasks. Unfortunately, similar to the way in which we become prisoners of an enduring past (holding on tightly to beliefs, habits, plans), we can also fall under the spell of breaking away from it. And just as continuity possesses an inertial tendency, sometimes there is the threat of an opposing tendency, that is, of embracing present moments that are attempting to isolate themselves from the rest of the world. Therefore, as a precaution against the improper use of these incantations, of these metatestimonies articulated during an exile that is lived as a new beginning (and as yet another exercise in avoiding the *principle of general credulity*), I will take a moment to look at several verses from the book *The Ghetto* [*El ghetto*] by the Argentinian Tamara Kamenszain.

Let us read a poem that is in fact titled "Exile" ["Exilio"]. It dramatizes the mailing of a postcard from Mexico to Buenos Aires. The very act itself acknowledges commitments established at some past moment. Someone sends a message to someone else in hopes that it might set their mind at ease. Beyond the exact words of the message, what a postcard sent from exile implicitly tries to communicate is, "There's no reason to worry. I'm fine." On the other hand, there is a distance between Mexico and Buenos Aires that no incantation can make disappear. It is the distance between two very different places, despite the fact that they share the same language and much of the same culture. I mentioned the acknowledgement of a distance between someone who sends a postcard and its recipient. However, geography is not the only distance. There are other obstacles facing this metatestimony besides the kilometers separating them. Various cultures bearing particularly heavy *present pasts* often sway from side to side.

> With Hebrew vowels
> Christian consonants[16]

16 "Con vocales hebreas / consonantes cristianas"

Here the poetic voice offers a portrait of the person who is sending this postcard written with a certain tempestuous Catholic-Jewish-Argentinian-Mexican hybridization (combinations of this sort are more common than we might suspect):

> crossing the desert at 40
> receiving *matzá* with a dry mouth
> lime deposits in my kidney
> sediment swirling from tortillas[17]

Despite the distance, the *matzá* (the bread prepared by the Jews before their exodus from Egypt) and the Mexican tortillas represent a certain community of ancient foods lacking in yeast. They are both foods of urgency responding to needs that cannot be postponed. Still, this portrait is not only made up of urgencies, established commitments, imposed wandering and hybridization, but also with palimpsests or merely those substitutions required by history:

> in the folds of each papyrus
> I scratch out Dead Sea
> I write Pacific Ocean
> I feel more at ease I place it in the envelope
> and I add on the back
> ILYDF.[18]

What are these verses trying to tell us? When exile is lived as a new beginning, many times one disregards those things that pressure and overwhelm the individual when exile is lived as loss or as resistance: the inalterable aspects of the situations we are facing, whether we like them or not, and our consolidated injuries. In doing so, we put aside the forced nature of many displacements and we pay no heed to the deadly seas and the heart-wrenching distances, to the substitution of one landscape for another or the demands made by irritating customs offices. Sadly, no "new-beginning incantation," no act of words, completely eliminates everything that invades and conditions: one's nature and personal past limit and decide the plans for satisfying one's needs. Because beyond joy and sadness, one must continue kneading *matzá* or tortillas in order

17 "cruzando el desierto a los 40 / comulgando *matzá* con la boca seca / restos de cal en el riñón / sedimento rolado de tortillas"

18 "en los dobleces de cada papiro / tacho Mar Muerto / pongo Océano Pacífico / me quedo más tranquila ensobro / y agrego al dorso / TKDF."

to survive the coming days and to uncover those camouflaged passageways between fear and ruin through which to escape. It is sometimes wise to send a postcard to yourself, writing down "in the folds of each papyrus": "There is no reason to worry. My bones have not yet given in. Nor have the lessons that I have learned."

With the appropriate perspective—accepting circumstances that are beyond one's control, while at the same time accepting, to a certain extent, history itself and its unending sequence of arrangements often expressed through habits and routines—the first person is able to endure defeat and resignation. Coexisting with injury and social and natural conditions that we cannot control, the continuity of the experience is also maintained.

Here we reach a third type of exile's direct lessons:

There Is a Time to Welcome, Even Encourage, Large and Small Discontinuities in Our Experience and a Time to Carry on with Already Proven Plans and Deep-Seated Routines

We are again presented with a lesson, but one that is even more strained than previous ones, in open conflict with itself. On the one hand, if we do not raise a banner over our horizon that announces: "another life is possible," as did the prophets of Israel, then there will be considerable risk of succumbing to either an addiction to loss or to resistance. Herein lies the urgency for one to sometimes position oneself in new-beginning situations and their various engagements: with awareness, with the body, with the present moment, with not understanding, with departing for self-reinvention. These engagements, if sincere, distinguish the introduction of discontinuities from mere transitions: one decides to start a new life in order to live, not only in order to live tomorrow. Moreover, each one of these discontinuities in daily life forces the first person to closely examine yesterday and today's potentialities. At least provisionally (perhaps irresponsibly), it is often useful to make oneself readily available to try out various ways of life. Or, as in the threshold created in "Space," it can be in one's best interest to restore the world's complexity and then, as an agent, whittle it down with each action taken.

By reconstructing the realm of possibility and keeping it in plain sight, it becomes easier to redeem oneself in the past and to plan for the future. In the past, I am portrayed as I was; it shows me what I have chosen among the possibilities that I considered available to me at the time. I am reminded, then, of missed or failed opportunities. Occasionally, this portrait can offer reconciliation: I end up understanding that my decision was the best, or at least a reasonable one, given the circumstances. Equally, concerning the future, an examination of the realm of possibility will many times reveal that there are more (many more) paths available.

On the other hand, welcoming the risks posed by the discontinuities coming from the ceaseless production of new-beginning situations should not obscure the fact that, although we are animals who give structure to time, we bear the limitations of a body and a biography as well as obsessions and commitments that are difficult to avoid. (No one would deny that we are frequently tormented by exasperating responsibilities that we cannot, and sometimes should not, reject.) The pathology of "being at the threshold" situations lies in what could be called *presentism*: the silly, albeit tempting, belief that it is possible in any place and at any time to do anything by excluding nature and history.

Presentism intoxicates with its hopeless magic. It unscrupulously appeals to enthusiasm—the blind excitation of subjectivity's demands—for the purpose of erasing what is there, the result of overloaded legacies (natural, historical). Whoever accepts presentism's obfuscations no longer possesses a body with a specific age and progressively fewer possibilities. There are no courses of action that have already been chosen instead of others that were discarded. In order to accomplish something, they ignore the conflicting interests and difficult negotiations that can result in painful sacrifices. There are no established laws or institutions. There are no powerful social groups exerting their influence every step of the way. How can we avoid these evil incantations that only waste words by tossing them into space with no rhyme or reason?

Incantations were described as invocations "when starting an adventure and hoping to ward off failure or curses." Is not every new beginning the start of an adventure? What is more, would not another way of characterizing new-beginning situations be to redescribe them as invitations to carry out an adventure, whether spectacular or intimate, public or secret, collective or extremely personal?

Adventure: an episode that deviates from the usual plans, with uncertain consequences and, more often than not, containing risks for the person living it. Occasionally it involves an extraordinary event. However, there are countless types of adventures, as many as there are ways of "deviating from a routine." Of course, when starting an adventure, a person must bear the cost of allowing a discontinuity to enter an experience: one must pay the tolls that accompany the introduction of new horizons amid their day-to-day tasks. Nevertheless, despite their price, adventures never cease to captivate us. By distancing oneself from what is safe, from commitments and responsibilities that are also sources of psychological and social support, the first person reestablishes its power as an agent through that momentary exclusion of such foundations. In other words, the person returns to life by (perhaps heroically) following their present desire.

The expression "present desire" underlines one important characteristic of adventures: the first person's relationship with this horizon of possibility becomes one of privilege and, as such, the present moment becomes a moment of possibility. It represents a privileged relationship with the present; in many ways, during an adventure one breaks or believes to have broken with what has already been attempted in the past. One also disregards the most reasonable plans and expectations regarding what lies ahead. As a result, in many adventures one manages to withdraw from the past as well as from the future. One often passionately (although sometimes with an increasingly uneasy pleasure) embraces the feeling of desire, which at that present moment is considered to be the only thing that exists or matters. (Maybe this is the reason why a romantic relationship with no commitments beyond that very moment, and which latches on to a present that is purely present, a present with no foreseeable continuation into the future, is (perhaps erroneously) called an "*aventura*" in Spanish.) "Burning the ships" as the saying goes, during every adventure a person looks to put themselves at the mercy, to some degree, of what each present moment experienced as a threshold has to offer. Consequently, in many adventures the temptation of presentism is great. How can it be avoided?

Perhaps when good incantations are tasked with protecting adventures from "failure or curses," what they are primarily attempting to defend against is the delusion caused by presentism. In what way? An adventure fails because it disappoints: what was believed to be stimulating at first is discovered not to be. An adventure might also fail if the dangers lead to the protagonist's death. I suspect that there also exists a less obvious failure. It might be what is alluded to as a "curse." Or maybe the word "profanation" is more appropriate. An adventure is certainly profaned when it succumbs to the *paradox of adventures that destroy themselves*: when the adventure is no longer an "episode that deviates from routine and usual plans" and becomes something permanent by transforming into a routine: just another annoying daily task.

We regularly find ridiculous illustrations of this paradox in desperate attempts to take up permanent residence inside the horizon of possibility, "the adventurer's adventure": the mercenary soldier; the lover of wild animals who becomes a safari guide; the professional gambler; the fantasizer who, in their excessive enthusiasm, disqualifies any intersubjective validation as having little value and, as a result, feeds their imagination with nothing more than their meager fantasies; the compulsive lover who only looks out for themself; or anyone who sees the world as a stage and, as a result, makes no distinction between effective political actions and artificial posturing, performances and rhetoric that resonate for only a short time. The *paradox of adventures that destroy themselves* is, of course, also a paradox of new-beginning situations. For this reason, initiating a new beginning can be confused with presentism.

Caveat: Although presentism is the most common curse or profanation of new-beginning situations, it is just one example of the temptation to determine these situations by assigning them unique content. It is not about avoiding the reduction of such situations to an (impossibly) pure "embracing the present," but also not reducing them to only awareness, to only accepting the body's wisdom, to only a struggle for understanding or to only departing toward self-reinvention. Instead, one must discover how these diverse engagements should in some way be coordinated during each stage of life.

Let us suppose that the expression "learn to introduce adventure into your life" means to be sure that from time to time there is a prominent location in your life for:

- engagement with the consciousness
- engagement with the body
- engagement with the present
- engagement with the struggle to understand
- engagement with the ability to be an agent and, thus, with the ability to reinvent oneself

But how is it possible to keep these engagements in mind "from time to time" without them weakening or even undermining one another? At a given moment, awareness makes itself present as a mechanism of narrative monitoring; we outline notions of ourselves and then proceed to complete them by telling ourselves stories, fantasies, plans, arguments. Sadly, I would venture that we do not always do so to our liking. For example, there are stories in which natural and social circumstances are frighteningly imposed despite us not wanting anything to do with them. For its part, engagement with the body is the experience that causes the conceptual content of one fragment of nature to overflow. At times, we thoroughly enjoy this fragment, while at others, during periods of exhaustion and, especially, of pain or illness, it is a source of suffering that we must helplessly endure… And so on and so forth. Therefore, only by ignoring the limitations that each engagement places on the others, as well as the limitations imposed by nature and history, is it possible to describe "embracing the present" in the same manner that presentism does: an evil incantation seeking to eliminate indisputable inheritances—those often-cruel stories of past and future days—in which a person finds themself, including their natural history.

Earlier anxieties now come rushing back, stumbling over one another. Where can we locate norms to which we can appeal so that subjectivity is able to work with the material of these engagements but still avoid each one's tendency to close themselves off? In other words, what can we do so that this third type of exile lesson, complex and elusive like the previous ones, does not disintegrate into opposing pathologies?

Moreover, it is no longer possible to prevent the appearance of *other* anxieties, some extensively more troublesome such as those voiced in questions like this: at this point, has our work with descriptions, readings and arguments—to recover exile's direct lessons—ceased to be just this? Has it instead gradually transformed into a game of various concepts and images articulated in the uses of certain words? Rather than being in the middle of a reflection or a meditation on the conflicting demands of subjectivity, am I not with each step becoming more and more lost inside my ever-burgeoning reverie?

Caveat: Let us not give way to censorship just yet. At least for certain stretches of the journey, *re*-creating oneself inside reverie can also serve as a way to explore possible notions of self or, in any case, to gather materials for rescuing absent voices, including those we do not realize are missing, possibly because we fear them too much. (Consequently, reverie—giving oneself permission to playfully imagine moving from a concept to an image, from an image to a metaphor and from a metaphor to an analogy—often introduces subjectivity's hidden demands, for example, reproachful voices making use of many bad arguments which appear to be irrefutable. Thus, interrupting one's own reasoning as it drifts among the uses of words or allowing oneself to be caught up inside a whirlwind of images, metaphors, stories... and their resonances, represents in some cases a clever method for avoiding the hypnotic power of arrogant reasoning.) Relying on this assumption—or perhaps exploiting it—I will move on from the idea of adventure, or rather I will manage to continue discussing it, but through a digression regarding the slight figure of the guest. But how? And why?

Let us reflect on the uses of the word "guest" that refer to people or businesses being accommodated in a certain place because they have been invited or because they are paying for that service. (Consider admissions like "I accepted their kind invitation, but there was not enough room in their house for so many guests" or often-negative discourses like when using the expression "guest capital," speculative financial investments that are quick to abandon a country in times of crisis.) A guest finds themself only passing through; they will decide to pause somewhere for a night, several weeks, months, a year, but it is assumed that sooner or later they will leave that place. Under these circumstances, a guest might not know exactly where they are when they wake up, and their first words might be to describe their surroundings in amazement. In some of these respects, the figure of the guest resembles, firstly, that of the exile, and secondly, that of whoever finds themself in a "being at the threshold" situation or in the middle of an adventure.

Additionally, by meditating on the figure of the guest, I believe that we will rediscover the dangers of many new-beginning situations and of setting out on too many adventures, as well as the anomalies of a person in exile. After all, are they not an anomalous type of guest (guests who have usually not been invited and who do not pay for their lodging)? For the moment, the guest's status as passing through prevents them from being granted any sort of rights, but also any sort of obligations that are typical of members belonging to a family or a society. Everyone else, those who are not passing through, those who belong to that house or are from that place, can receive the guest with indifference, with anger, with hatred, with kindness. However, the difference that exists between them does not disappear. A guest is someone who will at some point say goodbye, leaving the people behind to their chores, sorrows, worries and responsibilities. (In order to resist the temptation to make a profession out of adventure and to overcome the addictions that destroy "being at the threshold" situations in general, it is perhaps also helpful not to ignore the biological use of the word *guest*: a parasite feeding off the body of an animal or plant.)

In contrast to the figure of the guest and their possibly adventurous ruptures, we shift our attention to the figure of the owner—a figure perhaps misrepresented by excessive ceremony and significance. It suggests a center of continuity among diverse experiences: it is, with respect to an object, the master or proprietor, with its uninterrupted habits and dominance ("homeowner," "business owner," "landowner"). An owner can impose their will concerning what belongs to them: continually exercise their control. However, it is certainly a mistake to think that it is possible to use expressions like "to be the master of a situation" or "to take total charge of the situation" in a literal sense. This is another way of stating, "anyone who believes that they can take control of a social context just like that, even those which are more or less clearly defined (a family, a business, a political party...) is dreaming." Among other reasons, remember that the first person is incapable of exercising absolute control, not even over itself.

Let us suppose that the word "guest" can be used to characterize anyone facing a discontinuity in their notion of self; for example, someone living exile as a new beginning. It is equally applicable, then, to use the word "owner" as a metaphor for the citizen and their uninterrupted experiences: their obligations to the State, their responsibilities to a particular job and to their family, their religious and political affiliations, their personal habits. Using the homeowner/guest opposition as a metaphor can perhaps help us to shed light on—even reconsider—some of the tensions involved in this third type of exile's direct lessons and, at the same time, identify possible applications for this lesson in various fields, for example, in political life. Thus, is it not time that we make use of this third type of exile lesson and consider the possibility of participating in tense, precarious political practices like forming part of a society as involved citizens, but with an inalienable critical distance since even when living as "homeowners," we are still only "guests"?

CHAPTER 6

Words Say, Words Resonate

The next few steps will produce a rupture in the course of this turbulent reflection. That rupture will eventually return us to the disordered detours of the beginning and, consequently, to the transformation of exile's experiences into the materials necessary to rebuild *types of lessons* as well as *perspectives for learning*. However, first I will pause to review what we have learned, if we have in fact learned anything. In our reading of testament-poems, proclamation-poems and incantation-poems as exile metatestimonies, a typology of experiences has been developed: exile as loss, exile as resistance and exile as a new beginning. From these types of experiences, our reflection has recovered notions of self that demand that, in order to act intelligently, one remain keenly aware of the time in which each type is found: there is a time to be involved and a time to step away, there is a time to resist and a time to break with the situation being resisted, etc. It became immediately clear that the divergence between these times resulted in extremely precarious direct lessons. There are other causes—interrelated, but distinct—for such precariousness; for example, these lessons are particularly vulnerable to the intervention of arrogant reasoning. But what are we referring to with the repetition of an expression as anomalous as "arrogant reasoning."

Arrogant Reasoning

In order to explain the arrogant use of reason (or, arrogant reasoning)—a disorienting plague that often invades our desires, beliefs and emotions—I will take the vice of arrogance as my starting point. (This should not be confused with the insolence of "alternative Socratism." Insolence redeems itself by generating challenges and questions. However, when it allows itself to be infected by arrogance, it can of course construct walls that leave us blind and deaf.)

We frequently accuse someone of arrogance because we are irritated by their excess of self-importance as well as their contempt for others. Any object or event can be the cause of these conceited beliefs, desires and emotions—of this lack of decorum: staying in expensive hotels or driving Italian cars, growing accustomed to Swedish liquors or to words that start with the letter "i" ("identity," "imperative," "infrastructure," "interstice" …), having read books known for their terrifying content or never tiring of making poses or faces, being in a

 | DOI:10.1163/9789004385153_008

hurry and knocking loudly on doors. The importance that accompanies declarations of belonging with respect to one's "nation" and even to smaller groups (some political parties, some religious sects, some fishing clubs…) are notoriously welcoming of this vice. (One's beliefs—and occasionally the flamboyant vanity of being Basque, Yucatecan or Chinese, or the fact that several generations of one's family have lived in Boston, in Paris or in Buenos Aires—can incite, or at least have incited in the past, enormous arrogance.) Those who have been corrupted in this way view the careful discrediting of the other, or of all others, to serve as ample support for their own superiority.

And what about arrogant reasoning? Let us position this expression alongside others such as "practical reason," "historical reason" and "instrumental reason." Arrogant individuals observe, infer, discuss and act through the use arrogant reasoning. However, even the most unassuming people, the most upstanding political groups and the most responsible media outlets will also embrace this type of reasoning sooner or later—sometimes inoffensively, sometimes cruelly. I will examine three of its most prominent mechanisms.

The general presumptions governing arrogant reasoning are supported by disdain and a rejection of any beliefs for which they feel opposition or indifference.

As a result, pretentiously reaffirming those perceptions which discredit beliefs that pose problems (the most serious problem of all: when certain beliefs contradict the general presumptions) can quickly become a deep-seated way of thinking.

Furthermore, one of the consequences of arrogant reasoning is that the more or less systematic procedures used to reaffirm certain beliefs while discrediting others are transformed into immunization techniques.

If we reexamine the direct lessons in exile that we have recovered, perhaps it is possible to verify to some extent how these mechanisms function. We found that during catastrophes such as exile the inability to experience suffering and mourning commonly leads to the observer's arrogance and its aftereffects: desires without daring to feel them, beliefs without completely believing them, emotions without affection, expectations without expecting anything, actions without the will to act. Anyone who disdainfully grows conceited and walls themselves in (an act that often indicates nothing more than a lack of sensitivity despite calling it the "ability to put things into perspective") goes through life without ever being present. But beware, anyone who heads in the opposite direction is also succumbing to arrogant reasoning: the exile intent on clinging to their suffering and making it the "absolute formula of their being" does so by discrediting situations that disagree with remaining involved with their loss. Experiencing exile in this way has a paralyzing effect; it is no longer clear how to proceed. The rest of humanity, those who were not left behind, is reduced to "dark people who encircle." New landscapes are erased by the "unscathed whiteness" of everything that is absent. Making plans (those that are different from one's plans prior to exile, those that contradict previous plans or even those that have nothing at all to do with previous plans) suggest a sort of treason.

Amid the experiences of exile as loss—dissecting them, examining them—a new notion of self can arise: exile as resistance. Anyone who neglects or avoids the risk of saying no and its consequences—growing conceited in their ability to break so easily with the past—confuses lucidity with predetermined cowardice. It is no coincidence that one who has not proved themself during some bitter confrontation usually bears the burden of the fears that they claim to have left behind. Perhaps no one is capable of learning without having attended the school of social dissent at one time or another. However, anyone who completely gives themself over to resistance becomes a prisoner inside the fervor of subjectivity's demands and overlooks the complexity of the circumstances. As a result, they remain (aggressively) tethered to past and present suffering, if not to past and present hatred. (Hatred continuously intensifies the anger-driven repudiation that imprisons the hateful person and eventually poisons them with their own anger.)

Exile can also be experienced as a liberating new beginning. This notion of self teaches us that if a person refuses to call into question their desires, beliefs and emotions, then sooner or later they will become trapped inside the growing conceit that comes from passivity. Unfortunately, there is also a type of conformity that occurs when enthusiastically engaging in ruptures, in discontinuities: foolish praise for new beginnings that, on one hand, ignore the importance of nature and history and, on the other, lose their enriching character by abusing the simplifying passion of a habit. For example, when systematized, "new beginning" situations risk misinterpreting time by reducing it to a present, self-contained moment: presentism.

Let us assume that one manages to escape the almost ubiquitous operation of these mechanisms in the arrogant use of reason and, thus, from its increasingly overwhelming vacillation: increasingly devastating to the use of argumentation and its corresponding agents. In the case of exile, such an escape makes it possible to learn extremely valuable direct lessons. For example, one might execute complex and precarious practices in which it is possible to gain:

- The ability to be involved and, at the same time, to step away.
- The ability to resist and, at the same time, to break with the situation being resisted.
- The ability to introduce discontinuities into an experience and, at the same time, to support oneself with its continuities.

Such direct lessons in exile consider the contrasting attitudes required at various moments in life without ignoring or eliminating the tension that exists between them. In fact, these tensions are addressed head-on. For this reason, they are *tense lessons*, terrifyingly tense.

The way in which the tense nature of these direct lessons renders them extremely precarious becomes perhaps clearer if we consider how the essential material of each one (getting involved, stepping away, resisting, breaking with the situation ...) obeys addiction's maxim, so representative of arrogant reasoning: *More of the same is always good.*

For example, based on this maxim, one might reason, guided by a simplifying passion, that it is always a good idea to be involved with one's own here and now, that it is always a good idea to take a step back, that it is always a good idea to resist, that it is always a good idea to break from the situation being resisted, that it is always a good idea to insert more discontinuities into experiences or that it is always a good idea to maintain continuity.

Let us further recall the *paradox of persevering excitement*; the *paradox of practices that, while rejecting, incessantly reproduce what they reject*; and the *paradox of adventures that destroy themselves*—other indicators of an inability to manage the changing times in which one lives (of the blindness suffered by a first person facing constant modifications to the situation they are experiencing). These paradoxes, guided by a simplifying passion, also arise through reasoning based on the maxim "More of the same is always good."

Instead of indicating that, guided by a simplifying passion, "one reasons," a more appropriate expression would be: "guided by a simplifying passion, one rationalizes..." What is involved in such an operation? The word "rationalize" is often used to refer to a process of self-deception even through the use of valid arguments. Clearly, the voices inside us and the reasoning they offer are malleable according to desires, anxieties, motivations... that we tend to confuse with those second-order desires which, well-reasoned, make up our will. (Desires, anxieties, motivations... can easily develop into hurricanes to which the first person can offer no resistance.)

Thus, when the first person "rationalizes" instead of reasoning, they accept reasons that they would reject if they were put forth by another person. (The jealous spouse who shamelessly envies while claiming to admire, the terrified individual who continuously adopts a reckless attitude or one who disguises their lack of generosity with exhaustion or annoyed indifference are all pathetic characters who illustrate the use of the word "rationalize.") How can we fight against such observing, inferring and arguing typical of arrogant reasoning that, by rationalizing, move from one conceit to another, destroying the most valuable notions of self that a person can have—e.g., those that we have recovered as a result of tense direct lessons in exile?

As stated earlier, an approach that greatly limits the attacks from mechanisms of arrogant reasoning involves practicing the art of self-interruption. If memory serves, this art was introduced as a method—countering the temptations of arrogant reasoning—for placing us in the proper state of mind to hear victims' testimonies and, thus, to not disregard that "raw material of indignation." However, when attempting to prevent arrogant reasoning from destroying lessons in exile, we immediately discover that the importance of this art of self-interruption is, in fact, much greater. Faced with the varied functioning of rationalization mechanisms and their maxim "More of the same is always good," the art of self-interruption introduces an antitrust principle concerning our capacity to understand. Or, to use other metaphors, this art recommends a certain amount of fasting concerning our capacity to understand. One is advised to breathe in fresh air while tracing a line of anti-contempt that declares: "This is as far as I will go. Now, I must spend time listening to beliefs that contradict my own, looking at parts of my environment that bother and even repulse me, allowing myself to be interrogated by words that I detest, by desires that I do not understand, by emotions and expectations that I do not share."

Unfortunately, while the art of self-interruption is an unavoidable first step, it is still just that: a first step. It is true that we must engage with the "raw material of indignation" but, as with any "raw material," we must take a second step and process it. Something occurs with the tense direct lessons in exile. There is a second step to be taken in search of specific norms that might help to recognize in what time one is *really* living and, thus, to not fall victim to extreme approaches of getting involved or stepping away, of resisting or breaking with the situation ... One (provocative) way of responding consists in introducing the anticipated rupture within the course of this reflection: now that we have gained certain materials from direct lessons learned in the various exiles, it is time to examine *exile as a category of perspectives.*

We find that some uses of the word "exile" resonate inside many utterances. Resonate? The life of human animals has been infamously contemplated, examined, reasoned and sung, metaphorically associating it with a type of exile. So why then could it not be possible for different exiles or their experiences and direct lessons to also "resonate," not only as metaphors, but also as analogies that abstract from the particularities of a specific exile? Engaging with the resonations of words would provide us with yet another application, perhaps a decisive application, of our reflection's maxim: *Strive to rid social phenomena of their own inner boundaries and strive to do this again and again.* Let us examine this possibility.

Comparisons, Metaphors, Analogies, Abstractions, Perspectives ... On the Varying Resonations of Some Uses of Words Like "Exile," "Loss," "Resistance" and "New Beginning"

The word "exile" constantly produces comparisons, metaphors, analogies—some profound, some ridiculous—like: "My worst exile has been my exile from the sea." Or: "My life has been like one long exile from childhood." Or: "I often live exiled inside my fantasies." Or: "I am exiled inside my body." Or: "We all live exiled on earth." Or: "There is no worse exile than our exile from our mother." Or: "Without song, we live in exile." Or: "Life is exile from death." Or: "We all live in some sort of exile," and on and on, to the point of wonderment or exasperation.

We can complement the second maxim—*Be careful with words!*—with some new and possibly odd advice: *Be careful with how words resonate!*

Resonate: to prolong or amplify a sound. In much the same way, the uses of words also sometimes resonate because their dialects of allusions lead us to other words, to other discourses. This results in the production of anomalous speech, although often based on comparisons and metaphors that trigger new descriptions. However, sometimes resonations do not rely as much on a comparison—or metaphorical process—as they do on recognizing that the types of experiences denoted by some words are either similar to one another or examples of a broader type of experience. If this occurs, we find ourselves faced with arguments from analogy or abstraction. At least for the time being, I will consider analogy and abstraction as cases of possible word resonations. How can exile's direct lessons help us to better understand those human life experiences that reappear time and time again.

An Usher for Loss

I will revisit several examples in which the experiences of exile as loss might, and in fact often do, resonate. Clearly, suffering loss is not a situation exclusive to exile, not even to circumstances typical of forced displacements (those of the refugee, those of the émigré). On the contrary, it is a common experience—painful or happy, accepted or repressed—for human animals. Living in time implies loss. (And where else could human animals possibly live except in time?) Every person moves through infancy, childhood, maturity, etc. Every day and every night each one of us is confronted with an uninterrupted succession of everything that escapes us. People, opportunities, lands, desires and expectations go away. Sometimes those absences destroy us: loss becomes an unbearable burden. There are moments of abandonment when we feel we might not be able to carry on. Even worse, in the days following a loss, and even much longer, we sink to the bottom of those wells out of which we know it will be very difficult to climb (or difficult to even want to). Words lose their ability to produce anything more than testaments.

If we allow ourselves to get swept up in analogies, abstractions and other forms of resonation for words like "exile," "loss," "resistance" and "new beginning," how can we connect with the inevitable process of loss without giving up hope? Using the resonances of these words, is it possible to forge techniques that counteract the losses? Or at least, in what way or ways is it possible to avoid some of the many traps laid by using arrogant reasoning to cling too tightly to suffering and mourning? Without thinking, we tend to submit to subjectivity's demands with lesser or greater passivity. We have found, with regards to exile experienced as loss, that in order not to surrender to that slow suicide—brooding over what has been lost—one must know how to take a step back. That lesson resonates—it can be identified—in other spheres. In almost any situation, taking a step back adds dimension to the various losses: it positions them in relation to everything that has not yet been lost. Such efforts to gain perspective generate questions seeking to better define that experience; questions like: "What have you really lost?" and "Is what you have lost so valuable?"

When the first person asks itself questions like these, we can say that it has assumed, from among its many inner voices (both well and bad-intentioned), a friendly and invaluable voice: that of the "usher for loss." This inner voice, this hardworking usher, reminds it: "Look! The world is much larger than you think. It extends well beyond your pain. Outside of what you have lost there still lies everything else. Everything else is vast. And it is undoubtedly worth more than what you have lost. Therefore, it is important that you know how to show your losses to their seats, so that they do not keep getting in your way." Incorporating the voice of an usher for loss into one's thought is, again, another form of exercising the art of self-interruption—in this case, interrupting the feeling of resentment that is capable of consuming the world as well as the individual who is resenting. Nevertheless, in order for us to be able to hear the voice of an usher for loss, in order for its voice to break through the obstacles raised by deceitful, yet consistent, rationalizations, it must be reinforced. But in what way?

Let us continue examining how the diverse resonations of exile experiences and their direct lessons can generate forms of subjectivity that rescue notions of self which are completely unrelated to exile. Specifically, when facing devastating accumulations of loss and the temptation to prepare testaments, one way of helping ourselves to hear the usher for loss's voice consists in allowing resistance experiences and their proclamations, as well as "new beginning" experiences and their incantations, to resonate—to educate beyond the circumstances of exile by way of analogy and abstraction. The production of such proclamations and incantations is often among the resources available to a subjectivity attempting to survive: by appealing to the art of self-interruption, confrontations occur that show certain notions of self to their seats, for example, those which place too much importance on loss. (They also help with almost-imperceptible detours.)

The basic alternation between wakefulness and sleep represents one use of that art. It is not uncommon to hear or to make confessions such as: "I was too upset to keep working. So, I decided to lie down and get some restorative sleep so that later I could return to the tasks that my anxiety was preventing." One can learn from the everyday act of "restorative sleep" by paying closer attention to its adjective. *Restorative*: capable of fixing something that has been damaged. In this situation, sleep serves to recover lost strength. However, sleep is not the only discontinuity that is "capable of fixing something that has been damaged." Under the right circumstances, many breaks in our daily lives can accommodate losses and transform them into restorative "new beginning" experiences. For example, last Tuesday I was exhausted because I had spent all day dealing with pointless bureaucratic paperwork and meetings. Late in the afternoon, the doorbell suddenly rings. I open the door and standing there is a friend who, the moment he sees me, starts going on about a book he is reading. At first, I am annoyed listening to him; what an inappropriate, even violent, way of showing up at my house. Why did he not call first? But almost immediately, without realizing it, I allow myself to get caught up in the incantation of his words, one after another intertwining to sketch out the plot. Later that night, when after several drinks my friend decides to leave, I am more concerned about an accident, or an apparent accident, maybe a crime of passion, in the forests of Canada and its consequences many years later within a certain respected family, than the paperwork that I will have to take up again the next day.

It is possible, then, to learn various types of indirect lessons with varying degrees of importance. We found that this is done by using analogy and abstraction to extend the reach of exile experiences and their direct lessons. However, the resonations of words might not stop there. The types of experiences that can be reconstructed from different exiles, as well as the comparisons and metaphors that these types of experiences are capable of generating, can also be transformed into *perspectives* that can allow one to reexamine an issue, even with surprisingly fruitful results. (Sometimes, when deeply involved in the discussion of a complex problem, introducing a bold metaphor can bring about a change in perspective that makes plain something that had gone unnoticed during months of work.) It is also possible to build—with the uses of the word "exile"—a laboratory for reflection, for example, to develop oneself or to develop experiments like those encouraged by the second proposition highlighted in Chapter 1: "If exile is adopted as a perspective, sooner or later we will likely find ourselves faced with a dilemma concerning personhood." Or this other experiment that we will encounter in the next chapter: "If you adopt exile as a perspective, what meta-norms would you uphold to mediate between the norms of different cultures?"

Based on these observations, I now present a *fifth proposition*: *the various indirect lessons sometimes not only extend the reach of direct lessons, even complementing them, but also help to develop perspectives that will ask new questions and perhaps resolve or dissolve certain problems encountered by their corresponding direct lessons.*

For examples of this final type of indirect lessons, I will indeed adopt exile as a perspective and pause to explore culture, practical normativity and, of course, the second proposition with its stubborn dilemma.

CHAPTER 7

Nomadic Cultures and Personhood

At the beginning of this essay I described culture as "the cement of our social structures" in the sense that it flows between the many social circumstances and various manifestations of a person for the purpose of providing consistency to their life and to the life of a community. But how can that which we refer to with words like "culture" or "cultural tradition" function as the "cement" for all other social identifications and counteridentifications? To answer this and to search for new indirect lessons in exile, I will attempt to adopt the condition of exile as a perspective, that is, as a laboratory for thought experiments and, accordingly, as a generator of questions and answers. I venture now to present a perhaps shocking *sixth proposition*: *if we adopt exile as a perspective through which to examine a culture, however stable it might seem, large or small, sooner or later we will find out that it is, to some extent, a nomadic culture. Or, if you prefer, a culture with some form or degree of nomadism.*

It was for good reason that I suggested that this proposition might be "shocking" since, one might allege, ascribing "some form or degree of nomadism" to every cultural tradition sounds like nonsense. Each and every first person trusts that their own culture is a "second nature," as constant and reliable as their "first nature." Does not the general trust that we all place in our society emanate from the way it supplies us with a compendium of stable behavior patterns, trustworthy artifacts and institutions?

Let us return to a remark we discussed earlier: we live where we live. (Are we not inevitably wherever our bodies are? Does this not tie the body to a particular *here*? Are hunger, thirst, pain, anger, illness not all insolent reminders that we are from this place—that we firmly live where we live?) And even though nowadays we do not associate the realm of the sacred with a *place*—as was the case with peoples in Antiquity whose memories still held traces of the conversion from a nomadic to a sedentary life—that *place* still tends to define us from the very start; it shapes many of our behaviors and predicts a certain history. This is because each place is much more than a corporeal or geographical piece of information. It is fashioned from a complexity of desires, a tradition of beliefs and expectations, the dialects of allusions in a language, one or more religions, ways of eating and celebrating (even when that place is no longer a single neighborhood, but a mix of various neighborhoods). Therefore, besides being born into the biological order of "human animals"—we are not sheep,

 | DOI:10.1163/9789004385153_009

cats, horses or cows—we are all immediately identified and counter-identified with different social attributes.

However, we do not only live where we live. Ever since human animals developed memory and imagination, they have also lived in other, sometimes in very distant, places. The experiences of exile, among others, have emphasized that fact: Pedro Garfias, roaming grief-stricken through an English park, never grows tired of crossing the trenches of the Spanish Civil War. Where is Alberti, residing for so many years in Buenos Aires? In what city is Tamara Kamenszain celebrating a bar mitzvah? In Jerusalem? In Mexico City? In Buenos Aires?

"We live where we live, but we also live in many places." This declaration seems to be supported by the experiences of exile, as well as other forced displacements, but does one assertion not undermine the other? Once again, let us proceed with caution. To answer this objection, we must be careful not to confuse a *principle of presumed trust* concerning the most unshakeable beliefs and practices in a community, for example, with a *principle of general credulity* concerning those same beliefs and practices. We are again encouraged to heed earlier advice: *Be careful with words! Be careful with how words resonate!*

To begin with, let us carefully consider the word "nomad." *Nomad*: a person who moves from place to place, usually seasonally and within a well-defined territory, in search of fresh pasture for their livestock. It is also used to refer to a family with no fixed place of residence or an individual who does not stay long in the same place, a wanderer.

How it possible for a cultural tradition to have "no fixed place of residence" and, as a result, "to wander"? Even if by claiming that every culture contains nomadic aspects we are implying that every individual is always in possession of more than one neighborhood (those spaces that offer the possibility of memory, imagination and its artifacts and, nowadays, diverse forms of technology), this is not automatically a defense of cultural cosmopolitanism, at least not in any radical sense. However, this assertion is not only compatible with certain cosmopolitan concerns, it also reinforces them; for example, not allowing oneself to be deceived by appearances that suggest stability, if not immobility, within a culture.

Caveat: Stating that a culture has "no fixed place of residence"—that it "wanders"—does not eliminate the importance of *places* as an articulator of culture. It only recognizes that each *place* (including "psychological places") is part of broader contexts that influence its innovations, importations, adaptations and modifications. That is why—siding not exactly with a cosmopolitan culture, but rather with many cosmopolitan proposals, cosmopolitan concerns and a number of different cosmopolitan movements—I will discuss two assertions: "cultures are in a constant state of flux and overlap" and "change is the necessary condition for a culture." Let us take both assertions to be premises in an argument. Through this argument we can dispel any doubts regarding a cultural tradition's lack of a "fixed place of residence" and its constant "wandering," as well as pose the counterquestion: when have cultures ever had a fixed place of residence and not been affected by some type of modification? But let us take it one step at a time, lest our argument should degenerate into a brawl. I will now list potential characteristics of a culture.

Cultural Storerooms

Adopting exile as a perspective enables us to see that, unlike political entities such as countries—which have closed borders, customs checkpoints and armed policemen to guard them—a cultural tradition does not possess clear boundaries. (Those who deem themselves to be keepers of a cultural tradition vary between individuals who elicit either ridicule or, if endowed with power, terror. In the long run, however, in both cases, just like in vengeance, one is sowing in the wind.) Often, in addition to being mistaken, one turns to pedantry, or rather to plain nonsense, declaring that even though a culture has no political or social boundaries, it does have clear ontological boundaries. But we must insist: a cultural tradition has no clear boundaries—neither political, nor social, nor ontological (whatever the meaning of this strange word might be), nor any other kind. That is why it is so difficult to characterize traditions, and whenever we try to do so, we often end up with nothing more than a collection of stereotypes.

However, even if it is true that a cultural tradition cannot be fixed with the same precision as a biological classification or a political entity, it seems possible to examine some cultural formations—or different aspects of one cultural formation—in temporal cross sections defined by certain interests. As a reminder that we are not dealing with a clearly defined totality, it might be sensible sometimes to avoid words like "culture" or "cultural tradition," and instead choose words like "cultural formations" or "intersecting cultural formations."

A consequence of this lack of boundaries—boundaries that the intolerance of certain political systems manages to institute for certain periods of time nonetheless—is that in any cultural formation, we in fact find a fluctuating ebb and flow of "foreign materials," including more or less distant voices. Not surprisingly, cultural formations possess some form or degree of heterogeneity (which have only increased with new technology).

One might (apprehensively) speculate whether or not the use of the expression "cultural identity" is just a way of masking a puzzle of practices and discourses whose pieces often do not fit together. To begin with, the word "identity" in the phrase "cultural identity" immediately awakens a rumbling of distant and close voices. These rumblings—which are really just a confusion of social conflicts, personal rejoicing and resonances of both—also point to struggles between opposing cultural formations which often resist uniting inside one single "identity." This is the reason why so-called "cultural identities" are frequently reduced to shields wrought by our fancy and interests: stories effectively thought up in some political frenzy—like the steadfastly loyal war cries of "national identities"—or through uninformed, yet often still effective, projections. (Social projections and their way of reinforcing the limits between "us" and "them" come in different forms and are caused by many things. Sometimes they stem from a colonial attitude that confuses the heterogeneous reality of a culture with a despicable collection of stereotypes that point to, at best, the exception to the rule. However, we also find the opposite (romantic) attitude which extols those very same stereotypes as if they were the virtues of a magnificent Other that we are lacking and that we imagine we need. These "shields," these cultural identities, are forged—according to the *place* where we happen to be—somewhere between ignorance and militant selectivity regarding the cultural formations that we are attempting to describe—or to conceal.)

Unsurprisingly, cultural formations develop between cooperation and conflict. Thus, if we wish to avoid partiality as much as possible, we should try to view a "cultural tradition" as telling us conflicting stories or approach it by questioning its various translation processes (those generators of familiarity and strangeness) or use, and then develop, the biological hybrid as a metaphor. (In his work *Hybrid Cultures*, Néstor García Canclini characterizes cultural traditions as processes in which discrete structures, objects or practices existing independently combine to form new structures, objects and practices. Those structures, objects and practices are in turn the result of previous hybridization processes. For instance, in Latin America there are many things which are typically considered to be hybrid structures, objects and practices: things as diverse as a pre-Columbian collective imagination merged with New Spanish elements brought by the colonizers; the development of political institutions like "caudillismo"; mixed-race marriages; the combination of indigenous deities and catholic saints; Mexican dishes such as "enchiladas suizas"; the "chicano" experience; architecture proposing colonial courtyards with steel columns; collage-like advertisements juxtaposing historical monuments with clothing, beverages and sports cars; the fusion of ethnic or popular melodies with classical and contemporary music. Of course, it is not difficult to include heterogeneity or hybridization processes that are even more encompassing such as cultural traditions as a whole, beginning with each one of the languages—those dialects endowed with power.)

We know that sedentary peoples were at one time nomads. And even after many years, once they had stabilized their political, legal and economic institutions and customs, cultural nomadism did not stop: only its articulations changed. It transformed. Besides, since then there have continued to be forced and unforced displacements of people: great migrations due to climatic, religious, political or economic causes, violent conquests, evangelizing missions, colonial enterprises, adventurers and, more recently, mass media, the free market and the tourism industry. All of these displacements carry with them words, ambitions, lifestyles, goods, institutions, arms and money, among many other things. And many of the exiles have often played a singular role in the configuration of a cultural nomadism. This is why—I continue to insist—exile is so valuable as a source of information for our reflection. (To do justice to this singularity, we would need to carefully examine the contributions of the various exiles since Antiquity. But even if we limit ourselves to a very brief period of time—say to only a few years at the beginning of the twentieth century and to only one or two examples—we cannot help noticing that, both in Anglo and Latin America, the development of the sciences and the arts, including the beginnings of cinema, disciplines like mathematics and physics, professions like medicine and even the creation of publishing houses and educational institutions, would have all followed less-interesting, and perhaps even discouragingly inferior, trajectories had it not been for the Jewish and Spanish exiles.)

As for past colonial powers such as Great Britain, Spain, France, Portugal and Holland, they were nomadic since their very founding, much before their colonial enterprises. But here we might come across the following objection: if every culture possesses a certain degree of nomadism, is the expression "nomadic cultures" not then a redundancy and, as such, a useless concept?

Not at all, if we understand redundant concepts like "nomadic cultures" as disruptive interventions in discussions that seek to conceal those displacements. The fact that all cultures have possessed and will possess even more nomadic fragments does not imply that it is recognized. We often react with remarks like "This belongs entirely to me," "Only Ancient Greece—or the ancient Mayan world or Ancient China—and my culture have realized the loftiest values," "Only we know what freedom is," "Only by using this language in this place is it possible to ..." and many other idiocies of this sort. In difficult social circumstances—economic crises, unemployment, wars—we delude ourselves with such expressions to make the violent suppression of all differing voices seem more urgent. Once the dictatorship of arrogant reasoning and its maxim "More of the same is always good" has been installed, politics will not hesitate to recur to the firing squad and incite terror if it sees fit. (Let us not, then, forget that redundant concepts such as nomadic cultures operate, at least in some debates, as highly effective polemical concepts.)

But defending that each and every culture has its own form or degree of nomadism is not the same as asserting that its value corresponds to its degree of nomadism. Both are independent parameters. There can be cultural formations that celebrate destroying and recombining traditions, but which are of little interest because they are nothing more than pretentious kaleidoscopes. (As we have seen, fanatics of "being at the threshold" situations—i.e. professional adventurers—end up resembling fanatics "of continuity" through their tedium and foolishness.) Opening oneself to a broad horizon or frequently changing perspectives are not, in and of themselves, ways of attaining an embracing perspective—much less a penetrating one. Sometimes we only manage to produce an overwhelmed and distracted point of view. Conversely, devoting ourselves to the details of a small community is perhaps a way to develop perspectives that can help us unravel the labyrinths of generosity, bitterness, happiness, jealousy, courage … those dwellings of human life.

Of course, when this condition of heterogeneity and conflict in cultural formations—and their resulting processes of conversion, syncretism, creolization, miscegenation, transculturation and hybridity—is openly visible, it is often lived with fear, great fear. It is quite natural to feel that uncertainty is the rule of the day when what once seemed like solid ground has vanished, and this sometimes brings forth all the wild ideas that promise the restitution of stability: past or future paradises, something organically unified, an unblemished genealogy. This explains the renewed temptation to worship that cruel fetish referred to by certain uses of the word "authenticity." What do I mean by this?

If when accepting exile as a perspective, we take seriously the expression "nomadic cultures"—or, if you prefer, "intersecting cultural formations with some form and degree of nomadism" and their rumblings—then the word "authenticity," when not empty of meaning, can only have malicious uses when applied to a culture. "Authenticity" and "authentic" are words that usually refer to an unadulterated origin. In phrases like "This is authentic Peruvian craftwork" or "an authentic poncho from Bolivia," the term "authentic" is used harmlessly, as a synonym for "charming" or "traditional." However, when cultural formations declare—when they imagine—their "unadulterated origin," e.g., less affected by cultural syncretism or racial mixing, they are not affirmations of local color, but rather of an approaching political catastrophe. They announce the emergence of an overwhelmingly repressive culture, a cultural formation that intends to do away with any departure from its real or imaginary homogeneity by establishing a stifling *principle of general credulity* in relation to its own "unadulterated origin." When such "authenticist sects" become more or less powerful and resort to stereotypes, their "purity leagues" aim to suffocate even the smallest hint of any external desire, belief or artifact that they believe undermines their "customs," "good manners," "agreed-upon political line" or "blood"—whatever it is they understand by these words.

Hence the need to for us to dismantle authenticity discourses—the defense of sharp boundaries, of ideals regarding homogeneity and consensus, of delusions of immobility—by exposing their distortionary systems. Once this is accomplished, there is no reason why we should not concede that any cultural *place* incorporates materials that come from elsewhere: materials that have gone through a gradual process of transformation, materials that have been expelled or materials that have disappeared due to diverse economic, psychological or other causes. Moreover, we will no longer understand cultures or cultural formations as well-defined sets of artifacts, codes, disciplines and customs that should be preserved at all costs and that, for some unexplainable reason, must be honored by those unwittingly born into them. On the contrary, by embracing this new perspective—the perspective of exile—every intersection of cultural formations can be described through reflection as a type of storeroom.

Storeroom: a place in a house for storing goods or supplies; pantry. Notice how, since supplies in a house are consumed and then replenished or replaced by others, a storeroom experiences constant movement. Some foods are no longer available or become less appealing and are substituted for others due to the changing geographies, seasons, personal tastes, financial situations or market conditions. (Allowing words to continue to resonate, we could describe storerooms as being "beset with nomadism.") One cannot survive without some kind of storeroom, even if it is nothing more than a plastic bag we carry around in our hand. Similarly, it would be difficult, likely impossible, for human animals to get along without the intervention of cultural patterns. Thus, recognizing a culture's lack of sharp boundaries, heterogeneity and ever-changing character will not make it any less important to people.

Unfortunately, the use of metaphors like "storerooms" and the words "nomad" and "nomadism" involves many risks. On the one hand, we might succumb to the opposite, but equally misguided, posture of that which we are trying to correct, that is, to promote the idea that cultural formations must become a sort of market full of supplies that consumers can purchase according to their own tastes or money. On the other hand, we should also be careful not to suggest a ridiculously harmonious view of cultural intersections. That would be a great mistake. When we are considering the origins of cultural nomadism, we cannot overlook political and religious persecutions (after all, here we are trying to understand the lessons learned from a certain type of forced displacement: exile), systems of conquests or "defensive wars" (which are often only an excuse for the other type of wars). The storerooms represented by culture have not only been emptied and filled through collaborations and the social interchange of reasons, but also because of forced displacements, plunder and genocide. The very word "*alacena*" [storeroom] in Spanish is a remnant of cultural intersection and forced displacement: the settlement and subsequent expulsion of Arabs during the Middle Ages from what is now Spain.

However, one might dismiss all this talk of nomadic cultures and cultural formations resembling storerooms as just plain exaggeration. Certainly, the reasoning here has tested the limits of exaggeration and perhaps even given in to its many temptations. However, they are exaggerations of truths. Like redundant concepts, exaggerated concepts many times constitute very useful polemical concepts. (Let us not forget that to sharpen our thought, like when trying to wake up from a deep sleep, sometimes we need a gentle caress, and other times we need a good firm shake.) Once we eliminate the overstatements common to any controversy, our discussion can content itself with the admission that every cultural formation is heterogeneous in some form or degree, that it is always "adulterated" and it possesses a welcome amount of "inauthenticity."

As a result, anyone adopting exile as a perspective can no longer evaluate any culture as a "static totality," but instead will only see an intersection of formations that changes with time and that exhibits aspects ranging from the morally admirable to the morally atrocious. Thus, within a culture it is important to retain certain aspects, as much as possible, while letting others continue in their nomadism, so to speak, until they disappear—or sometimes even intentionally fighting to eliminate them. But what norms should guide us in making such risky decisions?

This concern had already emerged in relation to the precariousness of the tense direct lessons learned by reflecting on certain types of exile experiences. At that time, we asked what norms we should rely on when deciding when getting involved in a situation is a good idea and when stepping away is the reasonable thing to do; or, for how long we should keep up our resistance and when it is wise to break with the situation; or, what discontinuities we should favor to enrich our experiences versus how much and what type of continuity. In my fifth proposition, I pointed to the fact that indirect lessons can also help in resolving or dissolving difficulties found in direct lessons. Let us see then where we might find norms that can guide us through the dilemmas posed by cultural storerooms and the direct lessons in exile.

Two Kinds of Practical Norms

Through a reading of Kant's *Groundwork of the Metaphysics of Morals*, I will search for norms that might help us to keep the direct lessons in exile from crumbling as well as to evaluate our cultural storerooms. Let me explain myself. When at the beginning of these reflections I touched upon a certain kind of "present past"—traces of Stoic wisdom regarding exile—I also suggested that we read this revered book as if it had been written by someone in exile reflecting upon their experiences and lessons. This might have sounded irreverent, or in any case like a bad or misguided joke. To demonstrate why I think this suggestion can be taken seriously, I would like to propose a new thought experiment: I will sketch the general lines of a new reading of *Groundwork* adopting exile as a guiding perspective (and without any interpretation). I will avoid engaging with Kant's technical, powerful and perspicacious arguments and I will try to read him as if he were an exile who, terrified and in a rush to leave, had left the manuscript at home. I will also imagine the exiled Kant as retaining some rather vague idea of the norms he proposed in his famous book and reworking, even transforming, them from this new heartrending situation. So, instead of a "close reading" like the one I proposed for exile poetry, I recommend now a "distant reading." But this should not discourage us. When I pointed to some of the dangers of getting too involved in something, I mentioned that stepping away, and sometimes far away, gives us a clearer and richer view: scanning the horizon tells us where we are standing and reveals problems and solutions that we tend to overlook due to our daily, overly familiar, lifestyle. But, to which exile experiences and lessons shall we turn in order to support such a reading as this?

To begin with, the exiled person, perhaps like anyone who has been displaced and learns something from the experience, realizes that many of the beliefs that they considered as certain were only prejudices from their community, including some of what they thought to be their most secure "moral perceptions." The same goes for their "spontaneous reactions." For example, the sight of a person being tortured may outrage some people while others may remain unaffected, perhaps even justifying it as a means to some valuable end. (It is not difficult to verify this discouraging lack of unanimity in people's "moral perceptions" and "immediate reactions" simply by spending two or three mornings checking and comparing two or three newspapers, including those with similar political views.) Even the way character traits and emotions are praised or vilified varies from one cultural formation to another and from one person to another. In many cultures ambition is deemed positive and instilled in young people—especially in boys. In this case, ambition is described as a form of courage and determination for successfully reaching one's goals. But, does ambition not also conceal a different face? Is it not sometimes a way of provoking self-denigration among those in the presence of that first person who "has succeeded in getting their own way"? Additionally, it is no surprise that achieving one of our ambition's projects frequently leads to arrogant reasoning, which is reinforced many times by the obsequiousness of those who have not "succeeded."

Furthermore, many claims of authority are unable to maintain their sway once we view them from the distance of exile. It becomes clear how positions of great power are more often a result of their role within a social system, or even of pure chance, than of the qualities of those who occupy them. The same goes for many of the "solid reputations" in the artistic, scientific or intellectual communities. Even institutions that we have trusted since childhood—such as schools, political parties, the police department, the market, mass media—seem much less trustworthy from the perspective of exile, if in fact they still seem trustworthy at all.

We might ask, not without a certain sense of unease, whether there are any authorities that we can trust if there are reasons to doubt our most deep-seated beliefs and most instinctive reactions, the most esteemed character traits within a community, those people who have risen to positions of leadership and prestige, and the most established state and market institutions. Or more importantly, how can the perspective of exile, after having increased the feeling of anxiety all around us, help preserve the tense lessons that we have learned and guide us in distinguishing between right and wrong inside cultural storerooms.

Clearly, we cannot help feeling a general sense of trust in the information that we acquire from experience as well as in the most esteemed character traits in our community, in some prestigious figures or in the testimonial knowledge that we have been taught at school. But with respect to the *principle of presumed trust* it is important not to forget to underline the word "presumed." Consequently, we must be prepared—against the *principle of general credulity*—to pay attention to many of the particular reasons that are provided concerning those presumptions. We must appeal to the art of self-interruption, then, to enact the necessary arguments against this form of general trust.

So, if we seriously consider exile as a perspective for thought, then whenever a conflict or other difficulty arises in the general trust that a culture uses to offer its members access to the world, we should substitute the authority of reasons—of arguments—for the authority of cultural norms. How does this substitution work? Claiming that one has arguments supporting the belief that Barcelona is a Mediterranean port implies claiming that one believes to have the support of factual considerations, which are therefore valid for any person.

Let us imagine that a friend told us, "From very reliable testimonies I think I have conclusive reasons to believe that Barcelona is a port located on the Mediterranean. But those reasons are only valid for me and for no one else. I even know that they would not be valid for anyone who had studied as much or more geography than I have—or for anyone who had as much or more knowledge from experience than I do for having sailed throughout the Mediterranean Sea." We would likely respond to this individual more or less in the following terms: "You like or felt like arbitrarily believing that Barcelona is a port in the Mediterranean Sea. But if you had reasons, you could explain them to me, and maybe, with a bit of work and study, I would be able to understand them and share them with others. If your reasons are truly reasons, they must belong to arguments that *anyone* could share." If someone has arguments to believe that Barcelona is a port located in the Mediterranean Sea, then they must necessarily presume that anyone who is able to understand these arguments must arrive at the same conclusion. Moreover, for the information referred to in the expression "knowledge from experience" to be reliable, the one experiencing it must be "any person" or, at least, it must directly or indirectly relate information to other information that "anyone" could verify.

Something similar applies to arguments supporting action. To say that an individual is in possession of arguments for keeping a promise that they have made means that the individual acts upon considerations that would be valid for anyone under similar circumstances. When considering the validity of the reasons for both beliefs and actions, the individual, through the art of self-interruption, must attempt to dissociate from their culture, nationality, prestige, power and other attributes in order to become a provisional "anyone." Arguments—if they are to be arguments at all—are only valid from one *anyone* to another *anyone*. If we accept these (irritating) remarks that stand in opposition to our (assumed or latent) arrogant reasoning, then we can now identify an initial norm that should guide us in preserving those tense lessons and selecting which materials to discard and which materials to keep in the storerooms of cultural formations:

> Whenever you come across obstacles that make you question the trust you have in the values and norms accepted in your culture—either because those values and norms have been found faulty or because they conflict with the norms and values of other cultures—turn to argumentative practices.

We should of course be very careful not to use the kind of arguments that have been identified or counteridentified with a certain cultural formation or as if we were a lord, servant or some position in between on the scale of power in our society. Instead, the arguments we offer should be the arguments that "anyone," any individual, could offer. It should also be noticed that this first norm implicitly presupposes that people are not only sensitive to their desires, emotions, habits or interests, but also, under the right circumstances, they are sensitive to arguments. An indication that this particular sensitivity is real is discerned in the fact that there are at least some arguments to which a first person cannot remain indifferent, even motivating them to action. People would be driven to act by these arguments even if they did not wish to and even if they had strong feelings against acting or against the arguments themselves. Here are some possible examples: someone disappointed with the political and economic situation of their society finds good arguments to get involved in the struggle for change; having seen enough of corruption's strangling of democracy, they—perhaps unexpectedly—leave their (bitter or cynical) seat on the sidelines following the good political arguments they have found. Or, we feel we should challenge every government policy according to the ideas of the opposition party to which we belong; however, we find better arguments telling us it is time to break with past plans, emotions and expectations (that is time to look in another direction), and we do so. Or, a country desperately seeks to leave behind the inherited evils of a *present past* by granting a series of shielding amnesties; however, a group of citizens introduces arguments to the contrary, proposing instead that it is time that their society assumes its responsibility for past injustices by initiating a collective situation of "being at the threshold of a new beginning." As a result, the narrative of the community is then told again in terms of those arguments. When we admit the existence of these kinds of examples, we can accept that arguments by themselves can motivate us to act even against our emotions, habits and interests.

If it is true that people can be sensitive to arguments, then they are also able to distance themselves from their culture and their notions of self. Thus, people are able to act when motivated by arguments—a remarkable aspect of human nature. In some cases, they will act only on arguments. What significant consequences result from this "acting on arguments"? If someone acts on arguments, then they "move themself"; they set their own rules *to a certain extent.* This individual becomes an agent exercising *certain* control over their life and even, to some (rather small) degree, over their own culture. Contrarily, those who ignore the arguments available to them and allow themselves to be passively carried along by their own desires, the orders of current institutions or leaders, or the momentum of the cultural conventions to which they belong, surrender all control over their lives and avoid taking responsibility for themselves.

Adopting once again the perspective of exile, it might seem worthwhile to introduce a second norm both to prevent our tense lessons in exile from crumbling as well as to clean up and restock cultural storerooms:

> Whenever you come across obstacles that make you question the trust you have in the values and norms accepted in your culture—either because those values and norms have been found faulty or because they conflict with the norms and values of other cultures—remember that you are an agent.

To "act like an agent" means acting in accordance with the arguments that one discovers through the perspective of being a first person while examining the situation as if one were just "anyone" and placing value on the execution of the action itself.

It might be useful to redescribe these two norms introduced so far as ways of practicing the "art of self-interruption." We should remember the purpose for introducing such an art into this discussion in the first place. We wanted to become capable of quieting those voices already present inside our first person, products of identifications and counteridentifications with others, that do not let us listen adequately to what a second person has to say. We wanted to interrupt our inner voices in order to listen to the exterior voices also—to listen to those around us who sometimes challenge the perspective of the first person. With respect to the previous two norms, the "art of self-interruption" tells us that the first person must interrupt their very personal desires, beliefs, emotions and expectations in order to regain the ability to listen to the arguments that they discover by themselves when they behave as if they were "anyone."

It is not easy to behave this way. More often than not, as a first person we do not want to know anything that questions us or that opens us up to sufferings and injustices that we would rather forget, except when it can be used as an excuse to reaffirm ourselves, our culture or country against the horrors that we perceive (or believe we perceive) throughout the rest of the world. Sometimes considering the misfortune of other people is nothing more than a mechanism of arrogant reasoning to foster conceit regarding our own position, using displays of concern and sorrow to disguise our disdain for those who suffer. Herein lies the reaffirming effect of mass media on the individual or the community when it reports on growing tragedy "abroad."

Nobody can ignore how fragile and wavering our wills can be. Thus, if the first person does not learn to practice the art of self-interruption and does not make an effort to sometimes think against itself, it can easily fall prey to self-deception—rationalizations by which we try to protect ourselves from real or imaginary evils. Unfortunately, we are just as sensitive to rationalizations, if not more so, as we are to reasons.

Nevertheless, whether we like it or not, there are other people around us, and despite our best efforts against them, they will always be there, for better or worse, monitoring and helping us to come out of ourselves. I have already suggested that no knowledge acquired by experience is independent of the knowledge we obtain by testimony. Moreover, even the most distracted gaze of a second person is able to find tools to solve the conflicts of a first person, something that the latter—trapped inside its desires, beliefs and emotions—is usually unable to do. This is why sometimes only the interruption of a second person, either through cooperation or through conflict, can prevent the arguments of the first person from degenerating into mere rationalizations. How are these breaches in the towering walls we raise around ourselves possible?

Others are the first person's equals, but they are also its foils. As equals, the first person acknowledges them as bearers of desires, beliefs, emotions and expectations that are similar to the ones it finds within itself. However, the many second persons are in some way also different from one another, sometimes radically different due to their inherited nature, involvement in a specific culture and the person they have become. This is why every first person must face an irreducible singular *you* or a fuzzy plural *you*, both of which can be confusing, frustrating, surprising, consoling, loving, protective, deceptive, attentive and even responsible for life or death confrontations.

Thus, each first person is aware of the fact that not only is it vulnerable to the recognition or repudiation of others—to their collaborations and threats—but also to their actions attempting to destroy it. What should a person, individually or as part of a group, do when they are forced to face violent conflicts with others? Again adopting exile as a perspective for reflection, let us consider now a third norm for the mediation of conflicts between individuals as well as between cultures and their various formations:

> Whenever you come across obstacles that make you question the trust you have in the values and norms accepted in your culture—either because those values and norms have been found faulty or because they conflict with the norms and values of other cultures—tackle those problems with arguments that anyone living in a democracy could defend.

The exiled person we have imagined as rewriting *Groundwork* from vague memories—hoping to keep the direct lessons in exile from crumbling and to reorganize the content of the cultural storeroom—would now certainly like to make a few comments on these norms. Perhaps out of nostalgia for that venerable text or to keep those norms more present, the exile might call them by the same names used by Kant himself: the imperatives of universality, individual autonomy and the Kingdom of Ends. However, perhaps wanting to use less controversial terminology, they choose to call the first two mandates the "norm of arguments" and the "norm of the capacity to be an agent," and the third, using modern jargon, the "norm of democracy as a model."

In order to justify this final name, the exile might adduce, if they remember correctly, that Kant understood "Kingdom of Ends" to be the systematic union of rational animals by means of common laws. This systematic character intends for such a union to not only motivate consistency among the different plans of individuals and groups, but also to allow—like in certain kinds of democracy (or republics, according to Kant)—for those plans to support one another. That is because such a systematic union should promote not only mutual respect, but also collaboration.

A "Kingdom of Ends," a republican democracy that considers the interests and ideals of its members equally, does not of course eliminate conflicts or political, economic and cultural competition. Such elimination is only possible through the repression, or extermination, of voices, which directly violates the proposed norms. Consequently, drawing support from a series of social experiences, it would be reasonable to propose that the separation of powers in the State, together with competition between political parties and within the market, should be considered as possible mediators for all economic and political differences. Obviously, this proposal, like the many others in that great debate that is history, needs to be discussed, elaborated, modified or even replaced.

To summarize this discussion and to make explicit some of its implications, let me stress a *seventh proposition*—which, like the sixth, attempts to use indirect lessons to address some of the difficulties found in exile's direct lessons: *if when adopting exile as a perspective one reflects on practical normativity, one discovers that the values and norms that first receive our general trust belong to an unavoidable set of morals for deeply rooted people; they are the values and norms of a certain tradition and of their respective cultural formations. But when conflicts arise that the norms of that community cannot resolve, one learns that there is another kind of norm available: ethical norms. All ethics are an ethics for rootless or uprooted people, and the norm of arguments, the norm of the capacity to be an agent and the norm of democracy as a model are, strictly speaking, meta-norms.*

Let me make clear before too many objections are raised that the uses of the terms "morals" and "ethics" stipulated in this proposition do not correspond to the established uses. Indeed, there are no such established uses. However, as I use them, these terms are not totally disconnected from everyday life and tradition—they at least follow a certain etymology. "Morals" comes from the Latin word "mores," which means "customs." The expression "morals for deeply rooted people" refers to the prevailing values and norms in a certain culture that govern the treatment of oneself and others, but with one nuance: in my proposition, as in many traditions, such "morals for deeply rooted people" are understood according to the *principle of presumed trust* and never according to a *principle of general credulity*. On the other hand, "ethics" comes from the Greek word "ethos," meaning "character." This explains why the word is commonly used to refer to an individual's capacity to step away from the prevailing normativity of the cultural formations to which they belong—heeding their own *ethos*, their own character—and accept their own desires and emotions only as "presumptions."

To say that morals, in terms of morals for deeply rooted people, articulate the prevailing cultural values and norms of a particular community might sound like a preconception, but it is one that is worth making explicit. (Concepts that make preconceptions explicit can also liven up and even redirect our thinking, just like redundant and exaggerated concepts.) According to this preconception, to be born into a certain community is not merely a geographical or cultural piece of information. Why not? Notice how even when we resist events occurring within our community, we usually do so in the way our tradition has taught us—a way that is, therefore, inevitably infused with the values that are being resisted. Moreover, many of our desires, beliefs and emotions will likely be in agreement, perhaps for the rest of our lives, with the values and norms of the community in which we have grown up, formally learning them in school as well as informally in the "school of life," the school that likely teaches us the most. (I believe Hegel has this "school of life" in mind—its indirect lessons and the morals that govern it—when in *The Phenomenology of Spirit* he uses the term "Sittlichkeit," difficult to translate but which refers to the morals that nourish us and that we can never completely abandon, despite our rational efforts to adopt a critical distance.)

Still, let us not make the same mistake again by thinking that there are minimally complex cultures which are "homogeneous totalities" or "non-nomadic totalities." One can always find normative conflicts in every culture and their moral communities. And those conflicts intensify even more in a world of displaced people that, like ours, is a multicultural world. Unfortunately, in such a world it is not just a matter of some people covering their faces while others do not; of wearing hijabs, turbans, cowboy hats or Basque berets; of speaking English, Chinese or Spanish; of eating pasta, chilaquiles or sushi; of listening to Bach cantatas or the songs of Isabel Pantoja; of choosing to play tennis or pelota; of having short or long hair; of studying Avicenna, Saint Thomas or Maimonides … it is also about behaviors that *cannot* operate next to each other—let alone collaborate. Thus, if from the outset there are already abundant conflicts within a person or a culture, these will only worsen and multiply as irreconcilable values collide, sometimes fighting to the death. So what should we do when those conflicts involve moral values such as the rights of women or minority groups, the separation of powers or the freedom of speech or movement?

This question brings us back to the same unrelenting concerns that prompted our examination of practical normativity. For example, when conflicts arise what norms should we use to guide us in keeping, removing or introducing materials in a cultural storeroom? And what norms can help us to decide whether it is time to be involved in a situation or time to step away, to resist or to break with the situation being resisted as well as with resistance itself, to cling to our habits and routines or to promote discontinuities in our experience?

I will reiterate the answer offered by the reflection that adopts exile as a perspective: if we intend to avoid arbitrariness, violence and their cruel webs, we must necessarily first appeal to the art of self-interruption in order to genuinely see and listen to what is happening around us and, then, each person must frame the practice of their capacity for judgment according to the meta-norms of an ethics for rootless or uprooted people.

If we then consider certain aspects in a cultural storeroom to be problematic, we will have to examine whether there are any arguments that justify the elimination of materials, for example, if they go against the meta-norm of the capacity to be an agent. And something similar occurs when we feel uncertain in relation to a tense direct lesson of exile. Let us imagine that we want to know whether it is time to be involved or time to examine the circumstances in detail, lucidly comparing different points of view by using the most impartial perspective possible. We would then have to see which of those attitudes best promotes, for example, the meta-norm of democracy as a model of social coexistence.

Unfortunately, the relations between the norms of a set of "morals for deep-rooted people" and the meta-norms of an "ethics for rootless or uprooted people" are complicated. To begin with, nobody is able to sufficiently disengage from their own culture for their arguments to be able to erase their specific personal or cultural circumstances. But this is not just about accepting that "we live where we live." We should take into consideration something more basic: if we did begin by taking the contents for our arguments from the moral community in which we have grown, then where could these contents come from? (This is, I believe, one of Hegel's objections against Kant put forth in *Philosophy of Right*.)

At this point, I will try not to worry myself too much with the fact that this reflection on lessons in exile, which has utilized (and abused) the strategy of the detour, has wandered so far from its starting point, from the direct and indirect lessons on cultural nomadism and the uprooting of a certain practical normativity. Instead, I am grateful to the dynamic of this reflection for leading me to these indirect lessons and will now revisit one of the loose ends from the beginning: the second proposition and its dilemma.

The Dilemma of Personhood

If we recall, that dilemma was: *personhood is either reduced to certain social concepts (for example, certain legal and political rights and certain economic attributes), or personhood is independent of such concepts.* "Neither one nor the other," we might counter. Personhood can be classified as a natural order, namely the order of human animals. But does the adjective "human" not introduce an uncomfortable nuance within the animal kingdom that suggests social concepts? Let us consider then a different formulation of the dilemma pushing back against arrogant reasoning: *personhood is either reduced to concepts like those of the human animal and/or certain social concepts, or personhood is independent of such concepts.* And we might start to argue by asking complicating questions like: "Does what determines a person not exceed all biological and social concepts?" or "Is it possible that a person is nothing more than their biological makeup and/or the social roles they assume, or are they something independent of all that?" We know from our initial cursory reflections that there is no lack of support for either of these options.

Regarding the first option, we have already seen that both the concept of the natural order of the "human animal" and social concepts like the political and legal concept of citizenship—paper identities—do in fact constitute the necessary and sufficient conditions for being a person. In other words, since each person creates themself within the social roles they assume, a person is nothing more than the result of the ways that they are socially identified or counteridentified as a human animal. However, if we agree with the sixth proposition and accept that each and every culture exhibits some form or degree of nomadism, then we would expect that such nomadism would produce some form or degree of underdetermination within the social systems of belonging. This suggests that we are not hostages to the social roles we occupy. Instead, we are agents because there are moments throughout the fluctuations of a lifetime when we must decide which role we are going to occupy. (Sometimes a person is simply not sure what role they should assume: whether to be, for instance, an understanding and supportive friend who gets involved or a distant and impartial judge.) We can also face conflicts between different roles. For example, imagine an individual who is not sure whether to resist an unjust situation in their country as a citizen and active member of an opposing political party or to give more importance to their role as a nuclear physicist and move to another country with better working conditions. It is also not uncommon for one to experience opposing pressures and be forced to occupy different roles at the same time. Thus, siding with the second option, we can also add that the one responsible for negotiating those underdetermined social identifications and counteridentifications—often with the help of the voice of that "usher for loss"—is precisely each individual person.

But what exactly are we referring to with that resonating word "person"? Once again, we must not forget the maxim: *Be careful with words!*

Let us then initiate a new reconstructive effort focused on that notorious word. Should we exclusively defend the second option of our dilemma? Should we consider the word "person" as something independent of the uses articulated through biological and social concepts?

We have distinguished between two levels of practical normativity. The first level of normativity is that of a moral community that depends on a particular legal, political and economic life and, therefore, on cultural formations that articulate and sustain the natural history of that community. The second level comprises the previously advocated meta-norms characteristic of an "ethics for rootless or uprooted people." Those practical meta-norms propose that an individual be understood as both an agent and as "anyone." (This "anyone" has also been repeatedly put forth as the subject of knowledge.) But such a conception has motivated many criticisms, if not mocking or scornful reactions: can a person really be this "anyone," a ghost with no known residence? But, is an "ethics for rootless or uprooted people" obligated to equate personhood with that of a disembodied being free of biological and social concepts?

Against the first option I maintain that personhood cannot be reduced to biological or social concepts because it is a second-degree normative concept. But against the second option, it is equally important to clarify that those ethical meta-norms do not liberate the concept of personhood from first-degree descriptive and normative concepts. Why not? The contents of the meta-normativity making up personhood can only be the same contents as those making up the biological and social concepts. For this reason, it is useless trying to endorse one of the two options in this dilemma through defenses or attacks. *The dilemma must be dissolved, plain and simple.* What do I mean by this?

Through largely inherited materials—DNA, for example—each person accepts certain social identifications and counteridentifications determined by the customs of a community. At the same time, they occupy positions with differing degrees of power. But since individuals are not hostages to their own social positions—or they do not have to be hostages—each person is capable of acting according to meta-norms, albeit not always without serious confrontations. For example, one could appeal to the meta-norm that instructs us to participate in argumentative practices, as if they were "anyone," capable of modifying and even rejecting the first-degree norms of their community. Since individuals are considered capable of questioning their own desires, emotions, etc. as well as their social roles, they can be held accountable for what they believe and do and, consequently, they can be assigned responsibility. Even more, we assume that the ability to be agents in possession of responsibility is one of the characteristics—and perhaps a pleonasm—of those animals we classify as "persons."

I would like to try to dispel some confusion—to illuminate the darkness hopefully without making it any darker—by reexamining whether the experiences of exile and friendship support the second option of the dilemma, as I suggested before, or whether they help to dissolve that dilemma. When we come across a person who is in exile, we know that this person is not a citizen of our own country, and many times we are unaware of that person's rights, customs or financial situation. However, we also know that we are not standing before someone "naked" of any animal classification. To be sure, a foreigner will be identified using certain social concepts, but are they not usually much more than those concepts? Saying yes here would be either naive or deceitful on our part if we did not immediately clarify our answer. It is true that the rights enjoyed by foreigners are not determined by their belonging to a culture or State and possessing a certain amount of power, but rather because these are considered the rights that any person should enjoy. However, the *recognition* of those rights is certainly dependent on the political, legal and economic institutions in a certain cultural formation. (This is why, for example, those who are forcibly displaced continue to be mistreated at many borders, even hunted, as if they belonged to other natural orders.)

If exile initiates an exceedance of one's social identifications and counteridentifications, then friendship completes the action. All friendship is built and enhanced starting with a very spontaneous and unique feeling of empathy and from a pleasurable mutuality expressing converging perspectives on certain issues of common interest. However, over time those attributes that make the presence of that friend seem special often become less significant, if they do not disappear altogether. Those attributes represent irreplaceable paths for accessing the other person. But, what is it that we gain access to? The answer to this might sound a little disheartening at first, but I believe it to be the correct one: we gain access to a particular fragment of humanity, something that reminds us of how poignant, how essential the "raw material of humanity" is.

So, if I am not mistaken, the experiences of exile and of friendship can also be used not to solve, but to dissolve the dilemma of personhood. Successfully realizing this dissolution would allow us to claim that a person is that animal who fashions itself out of its own actions and narrations using both biological and social concepts. Yet, even while in the midst of acting or narrating, a person is capable of stepping back and reasoning in normative terms as if they were "any" human being. A person making the most of that opportunity can negotiate and examine their desires, emotions, social systems of belonging and even their most intimate imaginings. But alas, there is a lingering question that we cannot put off any longer. In order to locate such vast and diverse knowledge as that communicated by these indirect lessons in exile, was it really necessary to begin from such a particular political condition? Of course not.

Capacity for Judgment

To alleviate any alarm, I will frame my "of course not" with observations like: it does not matter from where the lessons come, but rather what they uncover and to where they lead us. Besides, as with anything there must be a beginning. And not only that. If we recall the opening maxim on ridding social phenomena of their own inner barriers, at some point we discover that even the most specific lessons regarding the most specific issues contain very general explicit or implicit consequences when considered through a sufficiently extensive perspective. Undoubtedly, much of the general knowledge that can be extracted from a particular lesson could have also been found through other different particular lessons. It is also undeniable that some lessons are more given than others to divulging general knowledge. And so, considering the enduring fascination that has accompanied exile and its frequent elaborations since Antiquity—in various testaments, proclamations and incantations, for example—is the condition of exile not a promising starting point for both direct and indirect general lessons?

Furthermore, with what we have indicated here, timidly but still with conviction, by searching for lessons in exile without accepting the barriers that commonly surround this political punishment, we also sought to reveal typical characteristics of acts of reflection and its use as material for our capacity for judgment.

What do I mean by "capacity for judgment"? Indeed, we are confronting a dual system of normativity: on the one side, that of arrogant reasoning and our desire for it to be porous in its application to argumentation, the abstract meta-norms of an ethics for rootless or uprooted people, scientific investigation and its theories, explanations and general laws. However, on the other side, we also hope for porosity in our habits, intimate experiences, labyrinths of desire and emotion and the possibility of being an agent in a specific situation. But it is important that we not cease being careful with words. That "on the one side, and on the other side" can easily be confused. It would be better to replace these words with "at the same time" because it is from within the disorder of those particular events that compose us—inside the callousness or passion of their everyday conflicts—where, if those conflicts are to be resolved or dissolved, we must decide when certain conceptual elaborations are appropriate: arguments, norms, meta-norms, scientific investigations. Therefore, if our capacity for judgment submits to the vertiginous simplifications of arrogant reasoning, weakening or suppressing the connections between theories or other abstractions and our most urgent needs, then it is with care and sound instinct that we must strive to restore them, as removed from us as they might be.

This vast porosity of course demands that every step we take be discerning; we cannot ignore that every situation is ever-changing and, as such, a risky process. Consequently, whoever wishes to confront life through judgment is obliged to take ownership of these unsettling words: "...there is a time to plant and a time to uproot what has been planted, a time to weep and a time to laugh, a time to embrace and a time to turn away ..." (Ecclesiastes 3:2–5). We must carefully hone our attention and never cease to readjust it as the circumstances change. To do this we will have to keep our eyes open, examining closely and without fear the times in which we live and what behaviors they dictate: what norms should be applied, what habits should we rely on, using what arguments, attempting what forms of coexistence. (Whoever wishes to avoid self-deception as much as possible must cast aside the tempting devices with which reason tries to immunize itself.)

The tasks undertaken by our capacity for judgment, its incessant efforts to prevent the deterioration of those beliefs standing in opposition to its own preconceptions, represent the most distinctive counterexample to arrogant reasoning and even serves as the name under which we can group the diverse methods of resisting it. (The counterexamples to an arrogant line of reasoning are not a debilitated form of reasoning—or even worse, a cowardly form. Instead, they correspond to a form of reasoning that, in order to operate without fear, is capable of braving many different risks, including violating diverse boundaries with its movement from one lesson to another, some filled with experience and others with perspectives: its direct and indirect lessons.)

In this sense, some common examples of our intervening capacity for judgment include managing the vestiges of *present pasts*; using various investigations, histories, verses ... to formulate typologies for those lessons that are precarious in the tension they contain; and revising deeply-rooted concepts like those involving culture, practical normativity and personhood. Because sometimes we must make use of any advantageous material in order to set out on our adventure, exploring the uncharted territories of justice, knowledge and joy with little or no support. The lesson is difficult, but necessary: if we do not give ourselves permission to destabilize our routines (including our theoretical routines), welcoming uncertainty and puzzlement so that later we can work our way through each situation towards a reflective solution, then we will almost certainly lose everything that matters most.

Clarification

There are some books that one decides to write, while others write themselves, so to speak, without planning them. We can even imagine that it is against our will that we do so—for some reason we defend ourselves this way. The chapters that you have just read belong to that second, impulsive type of book. I was invited on various occasions to discuss that strange yet steadfast alliance between exile and poetry in Spanish. As on so many other occasions, not knowing how to say no, I attended these gatherings and then afterwards quickly stashed away my notes inside the usual shoe box. Last summer I was offered the opportunity to give several talks on possible lessons to be gained from exile. With the help of those old materials, in a few weeks I had written up this choppy reflection. As we know, when starting out with slightly vague concerns, but ones which bear significant importance, if we give ourselves the chance, we can end up with unexpected consequences, far-removed, or seemingly so, from our initial intentions. It can be of some consolation to us to think that perhaps from this new horizon, we better understand the reoccurring experiences and actions of human life.

Indeed, the three categories of exile examined here—exile as loss, as resistance and as a new beginning—also constitute, as I see it, a way of structuring continuous/discontinuous human perseverance *in general*, not only that of those in exile. Furthermore, according to the way in which that structuring is carried out, these categories may describe it well or poorly—they describe it normatively. Then, learning how one should live implies establishing a *meta-imperative* or *life imperative* concerning knowing how to build losses, resistance and new beginnings as well as knowing how to interrelate those experiences and actions using one's capacity for judgment. One might ask, "What use is there in considering such categories, such abstractions as losing, resisting and new beginnings?"

Through a strategy full of detours, I developed this reflection around more or less concrete experiences and actions: ways of living in exile. However, there was also an effort made towards generality. This was justified by always keeping present—on the horizon—a strategy of passages, though it was never referred to in these terms. Such a strategy has fundamentally two overlapping functions. It is a strategy that encourages the passage from the concrete to the abstract and back to the concrete. In this way, the category of new beginnings found in metatestimonies on exile becomes a possible tool by reconsidering it inside other contexts of human life; for example, in personal contexts of emotional loss, in collective contexts of labor or political resistance … and in both

 | DOI:10.1163/9789004385153_010

the present and the past. But this strategy also promotes the passage from the factual to the normative and back to the factual; describing how one truly experiences a new beginning can end up being the first step in its analysis.

One might object, considering my intentions to be too wildly ambitious. Not only did I attempt to outline certain approaches to these problems by not avoiding the remnants of old stories, metaphors, analogies, fragments of poems read as metatestimonies and even reflections on culture and people, but I also did not shy away from a desire for generality. Of course, without subsequent reasoning—that is, without arguments that are expounded one premise after another—approaches of this type can often dissipate into thin air. But if we refuse to allow ourselves to participate in a little disorder from time to time, especially with certain investigations, we run the risk of being condemned to tasks that, out of routine, are guided by nothing more than centripetal movement, when not by repetitive and hollow paraphrase.

Bibliography

Abellán, José Luis. *El exilio filosófico en América: Los transterrados de 1939*. Fondo de Cultura Económica, 1998.

Alberti, Rafael. *Baladas y canciones del Paraná*, 1953–1954. Seix Barral, 1979.

Benedetti, Mario. *Cotidianas*. Siglo XXI, 1979.

Borges, Jorge Luis. *Fervor de Buenos Aires*. Alberto Casares, 1993.

Cavarozzi, Marcelo, et al., editors. *Asilo diplomático mexicano en el Cono Sur*. Instituto de Investigaciones Dr. José María Luis Mora/Instituto Matías Romero-Acervo Histórico Diplomático de la Secretaría de Relaciones Exteriores, 1999.

Cernuda, Luis. *La realidad y el deseo* (1924–1962). Fondo de Cultura Económica, 1970.

García Canclini, Néstor. *Culturas híbridas: Estrategias para entrar y salir de la modernidad*. Editorial Grijalbo, 1990.

Garfias, Pedro. *Primavera en Eaton Hastings: poema bucólico con intermedios de llanto*. Centro Cultural de la Generación del 27, 1994.

Gelman, Juan. *Com/posiciones* (1984–1985). Ediciones del Mall, 1986.

Gelman, Juan. *En abierta oscuridad*. Siglo XXI, 1993.

Gelman, Juan. *Gotán*. Seix Barral, 2004.

Guevara, Antonio de. *Familiar Epistles*. Ralph Newberie, 1584.

Hegel, G.W.F. *Phenomenology of Spirit*. Oxford UP, 1977.

Hegel, G.W.F. *Philosophy of Right*. Prometheus, 1996.

Jiménez, Juan Ramón. *Lírica de una Atlántida*. Edited by Alfonso Alegre Heitzmann, Galaxia Gutenberg, 1999.

Jiménez, Juan Ramón. *Tiempo y espacio*. EDAF, 1986.

Kamenszain, Tamara. *El ghetto*. Sudamericana, 2003.

Kant, Immanuel. *Groundwork of the Metaphysics of Morals*. Cambridge UP, 1998.

Kroch, Ernesto. *Patria en el exilio. Exilio en la patria: Recuerdos de Europa y Latinoamérica*. Translated by Alfa Weil, Ediciones de la Banda Oriental, 2011.

Laërtius, Diogenes. *Lives of Eminent Philosophers*. Harvard UP, 1970.

Lida, Clara E. *Calidoscopio del exilio: Actores, memoria, identidades*. El Colegio de México, 2009.

Millán, Gonzalo. *La ciudad*. Santiago, Editorial Cuarto Propio, 1994.

Moreno Villa, José. *La música que llevaba. Antología poética*. Edited by Juan Cano Ballesta, Cátedra, 2010.

Neruda, Pablo. *Canto general*. Seix Barral, 2004.

Nietzsche, Friedrich. *Thus Spoke Zarathustra*. Modern Library, 1995.

Ovid. *Epistulae ex Ponto*. Oxford UP, 2005.

Ovid. *Tristia*. U of Georgia P, 1975.

Peri Rossi, Cristina. *Descripción de un naufragio*. Lumen, 1975.

Pla, Dolores. *El exilio español en la Ciudad de México* (exhibition catalogue). Gobierno de la Ciudad de México-Turner, 2015.

Plato. *The Collected Dialogues of Plato*. Princeton UP, 1963.

Plutarch. *Moralia*. Harvard UP, 1976.

Rojas, Gonzalo. *Transtierro* (1936–1978). Taranto, 1979.

Scheffler, Samuel. *Boundaries and Allegiances: Problems of Justice and Responsibility in Liberal Thought*. Oxford UP, 2001.

Vega, Lope de. *Poesía selecta*. Edited by Antonio Carreño, Cátedra, 1984.

Vitale, Ida. *Procura de lo imposible*. Fondo de Cultura Económica, 1998.

Vitale, Ida. *Reducción del infinito*. Tusquets, 2002.

Xenophon. *Memorabilia*. Cornell UP, 1994.

Index

www.ingramcontent.com/pod-product-compliance
Lightning Source LLC
Chambersburg PA
CBHW031328230926
51848CB00001B/141
* 9 7 8 9 0 0 4 3 8 5 1 4 6 *